"Play Ball"

THE MCFARLAND HISTORICAL BASEBALL LIBRARY

1. Cobb, Ty. *Busting 'Em and Other Big League Stories* (1914). 2003
2. Axelson, G.W. *"Commy": The Life Story of Charles A. Comiskey* (1919). 2003
3. Ellard, Harry. *Base Ball in Cincinnati: A History* (1907). 2004
4. Richter, Francis C. *Richter's History and Records of Base Ball, the American Nation's Chief Sport* (1914). 2005
5. Lanigan, Ernest J. *Baseball Cyclopedia* (1922). 2005
6. Evers, John J., and Hugh S. Fullerton. *Touching Second* (1910). 2005
7. Rice, Grantland. *Base-Ball Ballads* (1910). 2005
8. Claudy, C.H. *The Battle of Base-Ball* (1912). 2005
9. Kelly, Mike "King." *"Play Ball": Stories from the Diamond Field and Other Historical Writings about the 19th Century Hall of Famer* (1888). 2006.
10. Anonymous and Noah Brooks. *The Great Match* [1877] *and Our Base Ball Club* [1884]*: Two Novels from the Early Days of Base Ball*, volume editors Trey Strecker *and* Geri Strecker. 2010
11. Green, Guy W. *The Nebraska Indians* [1900] *and Fun and Frolic with an Indian Ball Team* [1907]*: Two Accounts of Baseball Barnstorming at the Turn of the Twentieth Century*, volume editor Jeffrey P. Beck. 2010
12. Salsinger, H.G. *Ty Cobb: Two Biographies—"Our Ty: Ty Cobb's Life Story" (1924) and "Which Was Greatest: Ty Cobb or Babe Ruth?" (1951)*, volume editor William R. Cobb. 2012
13. Joss, Addie. *Addie Joss on Baseball: Collected Newspaper Columns and World Series Reports, 1907–1909*, compiled and annotated by Rich Blevins. 2012

BOSTON

"Play Ball"

Stories of the Diamond Field and Other Historical Writings about the 19th Century Hall of Famer

by MIKE "KING" KELLY

McFarland Historical Baseball Library, 9
Gary Mitchem *and* Mark Durr, *Editors*

McFarland & Company, Inc., Publishers
Jefferson, North Carolina, and London

Frontispiece: An illustration depicting Mike "King" Kelly in uniform for the National League's Boston club.

LIBRARY OF CONGRESS CATALOGUING-IN-PUBLICATION DATA

Kelly, Michael J., 1857–1894.
Play ball: stories of the diamond field and other historical writings about the 19th century hall of famer / by Mike Kelly.
[Gary Mitchem and Mark Durr, series editors]
p. cm. — (McFarland historical baseball library ; 9)
Includes index.
[Originally published: Boston : Press of Emery & Hughes, c1888.]
[With new editors' note.]

ISBN 0-7864-2363-3 (softcover : 50# alkaline paper) ∞

1. Kelly, Michael J., 1857–1894. 2. Baseball players—United States—Biography. 3. Baseball—United States—History—19th century. I. Mitchem, Gary. II. Durr, Mark. III. Title. IV. Series.
GV865.K52K45 2006
796.357092—dc22 2006004316

British Library cataloguing data are available

On the cover: Mike "King" Kelly (National Basebal Hall of Fame Library, Cooperstown, NY)

Manufactured in the United States of America

McFarland & Company, Inc., Publishers
Box 611, Jefferson, North Carolina 28640
www.mcfarlandpub.com

Table of Contents

Editors' Note

Though he died in 1894, Michael J. Kelly had much in common with the modern athlete-as-celebrity. His 1887 signing with the Boston Beaneaters made front page news after the club paid an unprecedented $10,000 for his release from Chicago and another $5,000 for his salary. His relationships with management, coaches, and fellow players was likewise public, as he used the newspapers both to negotiate with and antagonize the people around him. On the field, he delighted in baiting umpires and opponents, and he circumvented the rules at every opportunity; off the field, he cultivated a second career, in the theater, that kept him in the public eye. All of this made Kelly an irresistible figure. Sportswriters sought him out, related his stories and reported on his every move. That Kelly and others might imagine his autobiography could be profitable is no surprise.

Baseball's first player autobiography, "*Play Ball*" was released in the spring of 1888, with a first printing reportedly as large as 25,000 copies. By July, Kelly claimed that royalties already amounted to $1,500, a sum that would represent thousands of copies sold (at 25 cents each) in just a few months. The 86-page book purports to be a ballplayer's dutiful response to the public clamor for information. Kelly may have had a hand in the writing. The uneven tone—sometimes neutral, sometimes wryly conspiratorial, sentimental in other spots—and the narrative's erratic shifts from biographical chapters to apparently random thematic topics suggest that unlike ballplayers of the 1910s who worked with professionals such as John Wheeler, Kelly could have been directly involved. The popular belief today is that one of two Boston-area sportswriters either ghostwrote "*Play Ball*" or edited the manuscript and contributed the book's unsigned preface. Jacob Morse is the leading candidate. Well-known in baseball circles, Morse was a reporter for the *Boston Herald* and had written one of the early histories of the game, *Sphere and Ash*. He would later edit *Baseball Magazine*. More recently, biographer Harold Rosenberg uncovered evidence that points toward *Boston Globe* reporter Jack Drohan, a friend of the player.

The book's title is of interest for a couple of reasons. Today's reader might assume that "Play Ball" refers to the umpire's command. According to *The New Dickson Baseball Dictionary*, however, the phrase wasn't used in that sense until 1901. In commenting on the book and its title, Howard Rosenberg cites this line from an 1885 article: "Mike Kelly's war cry is 'Play Ball.'" But a broader sense of the phrase, familiar now as then, was also in general use, as demonstrated in this excerpt from a game summary published in the May 22, 1886, *Chicago Daily*: "[Pitcher Hugh "One Arm"] Daily seemed to let down completely, and his lack of heart was so noticeable that the spectators called out to him 'play ball.'" This exhortation to play with determination and vigor, which Kelly was in fact known to direct at the opposition, evokes the hard-charging style Kelly was famous for.

The front cover of the first edition, published in 1888 by Emery & Hughes.

The subtitle has long been a point of uncertainty, as well. The book's cover employs one phrase, "Stories of the Ball Field," while the title page and running heads indicate that it should be "Stories of the Diamond Field." The editors of the McFarland edition have chosen the second of these possibilities, which avoids the repetition of *ball* and nicely ties the book to its era, when *diamond field* was used metonymously for *base ball*.

The McFarland edition of "Play Ball" includes four appendices of historical interest. Appendix A is a chapter from *Wright & Ditson's Book on Batting, Pitching, Fielding, and Base Running* (1884). Ostensibly, the first three pages are written by Kelly; the pages that follow establish Kelly's authority on the subject of baserunning and feature diagrams of a dark-haired mustachioed player sliding, leading off a base, and running. Appendix B is Billy Boxer's "King Kelly, the Famous Catcher" (1892), a 16-page biography published as part of Street & Smith's New York Five Cent Library. Probably no baseball song, with the exception of "Take Me Out to the Ball Game," is as widely known as "Slide, Kelly, Slide!," the lyrics and sheet music for which make up Appendix C. Finally, Appendix D includes select articles about Kelly from the newspapers of his day. They provide examples of Kelly's outrageous (and often humorous) on-field behavior, his easy rapport with the writers and knack for story-telling, the general response to his 1887 signing with Boston and to his death in 1894, and other noteworthy episodes from Kelly's career.

The text of the 1887 book is exactly reproduced for the McFarland edition. Conventions of spelling and punctuation have not been updated, and any stylistic peculiarities or historical inaccuracies remain. The pagination has been adjusted to fit series specifications, and some photographs have been re-sized, their placement minimally affected. For the reader's convenience, the running heads on right-hand pages now indicate the chapter number. In the original edition, right- and left-hand pages carried the same running head: "'Play Ball': Stories of the Diamond Field." The editors' note, four appendices, and an index have been added.

The editors gratefully acknowledge the National Baseball Hall of Fame Library and Museum, for the appended Billy Boxer biography and sheet music for "Slide, Kelly, Slide!"; William Chase and the Charles W. Mears Baseball Collection at the Cleveland Public Library, for the chapter from *Wright & Ditson's Book on Batting, Pitching, Fielding, and Base Running*; Andy McCue and the SABR Bibliography Committee, for their continued help with indexing; Howard Rosenberg, whose greatly detailed *Cap Anson II* proved helpful; and Pam Mitchem, instructor and archivist at Appalachian State University, for securing a copy of "*Play Ball.*"

Gary Mitchem *and* Mark Durr

PLAY BALL

Stories of the Diamond Field

To the thousands of American people who annually grow
excited and cheer on their favorite players to victory:
to the ball players of America:
and to the small boy who does so much to uphold the game:
this book is dedicated by the author.

Preface*

As a rule, the preface of a book is dull, and there are very few people energetic enough to wade through it. Therefore, when Mr. Kelly requested me to write a preface to his little book, I made up my mind that it would be brief, and to the point. The man himself is so well known to the great American public, that one word of introduction about him is hardly necessary. For a number of years he has stood at the head of his profession. He got there by hard work, and he holds the position by a wonderful display of physical vitality. He has done much to improve the interests in our national sport, and on all sides he is hailed as "The King of the Diamond," a title which he richly deserves.

Mr. Kelly's work on the base ball field has been simply wonderful. Not only is he a good, safe batter, but he is regarded as the very best base runner in this country. Combined with these valuable requisites in the make-up of a ball player, he is one of the greatest all-around players in this country. His record at the finish of the season might, perhaps, not be as good as that of other players, but it must be remembered that he is not a record player. He is a winning player, and always plays for his nine to win. Kelly on the ball field is much better known than Kelly in private life. On the ball field he is a dashing, go-ahead, get-there, and inspires his fellows with the greatest confidence. He is cautious, yet at the same time he is bold. He is quick to see a point, and quicker to take advantage of it. When other men would stop to think in a game, he would be acting, and generally acting for the best. Kelly has an immense amount of energy, and, when on the ball field, he seldom rests. How wonderfully clever is his coaching from the first bag

*The preface to *"Play Ball!"*, contributed by an unidentified writer, is what most today would term a foreword. Unsigned by the author, it is most often attributed by historians to either Jacob Morse or Jack Drohan.

when a run is needed! As a base runner he has few equals. He has a record of having covered the bases in just fifteen seconds.

Mr. Kelly won his great reputation while a member of the Chicago club. While there his great head-work, his bold but successful tricks, his wonderful base running, and his timely batting, all assisted in winning many championship games for his club. At present he is a member of the Boston club. It cost the Boston management just $15,000 to secure him for a year. Of this sum, $10,000 was paid to the Chicago club for his release, and $5,000 for the first year's salary. The salary and premium is just about one and one-half as great as that received by the chief justices of the United States, and five times as large as the amount received by the governors of many States. It will be remembered that for this salary, Mr. Kelly works but a few months in the summer season.

Off the ball field, as well as on, Mr. Kelly is a great favorite. He is personally acquainted with many prominent men, and has more friends than any man in his profession. His cheery, open-hearted nature is almost a proof against enmity,—unless, perhaps, some does exist in the base ball ranks because of professional jealousy. He is generous with his money; and no comrade or acquaintance, in misfortune, ever applied to him for aid and went away empty handed. An intelligent, agreeable conversationalist, he always has something good to say, and he knows just how to say it. Blessed with an original personality, he finds many imitators, especially in his profession. If Kelly originates today, his idea is copied tomorrow.

In his book, "Play Ball," Mr. Kelly doesn't claim any literary finish. He simply has a series of stories to relate, and he tells them in his own way. What could be better. In base ball, he doesn't play to win the applause of the grand stand; he plays heart and soul to please the masses. So it is in this book. It is intended for the American people, both old and young. It will be found as interesting to the overworked lawyer, who closes his office early on a summer afternoon to see a ball game, as it is to the American small boy, who "hooks Jack," and witnesses the game from behind a knot-hole in the fence. It will be found particularly interesting coming from the "king of the ball field." In closing I can but say, "Long live the king!" May his book be as successful with the lovers of the national sport, as its author has been on the diamond field.

Boston, April 1, 1888

Chapter I

There are so many exciting incidents in the life of a ball player, that it is almost impossible for one to put them on paper. A ball player is a busy individual in the summer months, and in the winter very often he has but little to do. Therefore, when the idea of writing a few reminiscences was suggested to me, I thought it an excellent idea. Here at Hyde Park on the Hudson, where I spend the winter months, one has plenty of time for literary work. There isn't a great deal to do here in winter. There is plenty of ice boating and "sliding" down the big hill,—"tobogganing" they call it in the big cities, but "sliding" is good enough for Hyde Park,—the entertainments and dances at the engine-house, the billiard tournament at the Hyde Park Club, a most excellent club for young men, founded by Archibald Rogers a few years since, and the meeting of the village gossips at "Pop" Hornung's. So one can see that writing is a most agreeable change from these pastimes.

I will not endeavor to tire my readers with a history of the game in this country. Abler pens than mine have done that. I will simply relate some of my experiences on the diamond field, and give a brief sketch of my career.

There are so many interesting things which occur in the course of a season, that unless one has a particularly retentive memory, he is apt to be at a loss just to know when to begin and where to stop. In these articles I will not bore my readers by discussing rules or the principles of the game. Those of you who have seen a base ball game know just how its played, and what the rules are. Those of you who have never witnessed a game of ball should go, at the first opportunity next season. I am willing to wager that after looking at three or four games you will become a regular fiend. I have known men to forsake their business day after day to see their favorite clubs at work. There is excitement enough in two hours to last the ordinary man for as many days.

Many times have I been asked the question, "To what do you ascribe the great popularity of base ball?" This, seems to me, can be answered in just two words, "The excitement." People go to see games because they love excitement and love to be worked up. That is one reason why I believe in "kicking" now and then on the diamond. It may be all right for the newspapers to say that "base ball will become more popular when played without kicking." I disagree entirely with these authorities on this subject. Look at the Chicago Base Ball Club. It has been the most successful in this country. Why? One good reason because they are "chronic kickers," and people flock to see them to witness the sport. You won't find the ordinary man going out to a base ball field when it's 80° in the shade to see two clubs play ball for a couple of hours, without a word being said on either side. The people who go to ball games want good playing, with just enough kicking to make things interesting thrown in.

Of course, because of being the $10,000 beauty, and all that sort of thing, there was more or less excitement regarding my appearance with the Boston club last season. In some towns they had an idea that I was a sort of "Jumbo." Down in Hartford I remember playing a good game, and keeping pretty quiet all the way through it. Yet I played ball just as good as I ever did before. At the conclusion of the game I heard a conversation between two men.

One said, "So that is Kelly, is it? Well, what do you think of him?"

His partner replied, "Well, I firmly believe that he is an overrated player. Why, he didn't kick a bit. He can't play ball." You see he wanted more kicking and less ball playing. There wasn't excitement enough in the game, and it made him very sore, indeed.

All of which convinces me that a little kicking now and then will greatly please the best of men.

In this book I will, by request of a good many young men throughout the country, give a few hints on training. There are one hundred and one different ideas as to how a man should train. Some of them are good, and some of them are anything but good.

Chapter II

Whether it's of any particular interest or not I do not know, but as a matter of fact, I was born in Troy, N. Y., Dec. 31, 1857. My father enlisted among the first citizens of Troy, and did his duty as a soldier for three years — the term of his enlistment. He made a good soldier, too, and he liked it so well that at the end of his three years' enlistment he again joined Uncle Sam's forces, and served his flag until the war was over. Meanwhile I grew up a healthy, good-sized boy, and my good mother sent me to school in Troy when I was but five years old. She was desirous that I should receive a good education — a trait which runs through almost every parent who comes from the little green isle across the sea. They may not have had the advantages for an education themselves,— British misrule prevents that,— but they know the value of education, and feel that their sons and daughters shall receive their share of it in this great country of ours. When the war was over my father was stationed at Washington, so the family moved there. There were two generals I saw there in a parade of some sort when I was a boy, and I never shall forget their magnificence. They were General McClellan and General Kilpatrick. So much gold and gold lace I never saw before. They were simply magnificent. For years I remembered them, and it was the ambition of my life to go and do likewise. Well, there never was another war, to give me the desired opportunity. I pray God there never shall be. We are all citizens of one grand, glorious country. We all should work for the common good, and have our glorious country lead the nations of the world, which it certainly does.

I was sent to school again in Washington, and as I grew older I grew stronger, and so did my love for out-door sports. At nine years I could outrun any boy in the school, and a year later I made my first appearance as a base ball player.

Base ball in those days was a little bit different from the game of the present. The boys used to play "burn ball." If you were hit by the ball before reaching the base, you were out. Many a time have I been hit in the small of the back, and for a moment imagined that my back was broken.

I played my first real games in Washington as a member of a regularly organized club. I went in with the Keystones, and played in various positions.

One of the very best players in the team at that time was Dave Walling. Dave was a great ball player for a boy. Not only could he bat well, but he ran bases in great shape, and could play almost each and every position in the field in a most acceptable manner. I always said that if he stuck to it he would become a great ball player. But he wouldn't stick. He got stage-struck, and doubled up with Reynolds, who was also a Washington boy. Under the names of Reynolds and Walling, these two made quite a reputation on the variety stage. I have always felt bad for Walling. The stage gained a good actor, and the ball field lost a great player, and don't you forget it.

Ill health compelled my father to leave the army, and we moved to Paterson, N. J., where I saw for the first time the "red mud" for which that State is so famous. I liked the color of it at first, but after being caught in a bad rain-storm one night, and getting mud all over me from top to bottom, I had no special regard left for the aesthetic color. My father's health didn't continue to improve any, and we had not been in Paterson very long before he passed over to the great silent majority. My mother followed him not long after. God bless them both, I shall forever cherish and bless their memory.

My boyhood days in Paterson were just the same as is usually spent by boys. In my more youthful days, out-door sports occupied most of my time after school-hours. Like many of the college youth of the present day, I didn't go in very strong for study, but I was a great hand for the sport. "Jim" McCormick, now of the Pittsburg club, was one of my earliest comrades in Paterson. We always agreed upon the proper kinds of sport, and our great admiration for Joe Start bound us more strongly together. We did not know whether we would become actors, ball players, or engineers on the railroad. These, to us, were the ideal professions. We would talk for hours and hours over our whittling sticks talking over the glorious future which awaited us.

Finally we resolved to go into the theatrical business. Mac's father had a good-sized cellar in his house, and here we erected our theatre. We had a disagreement on the opening bill. Mac wanted the performance to be "Jack Sheppard," my ideal was "Dick Turpin." Well, Mac had his way. His father owned the theatre. I wanted to play Jack, but again Mac had his way. He played the robber and I made my appearance as "Jonathan Wild, the thief taker." We opened the cellar, and to use a professional saying, "turned people away." There was just forty-five boys in the house, which meant that the proceeds were just forty-five cents. The play went along all right until near the close. Then "Jack Sheppard" is hanged. The rope was put around Mac's neck, and as the cheap curtains were drawn together the audience saw Jack pushed off the block he stood on. Jack grew black and blue in the face, and were it not for the arrival of McCormick senior on the stage, perhaps the present great pitcher of the Pittsburg club would never have been heard of. "Jack Sheppard" was cut down, and for a couple of days he was a very sick robber. He was willing that I should play Jack after that. But I wasn't. I didn't care to take any chances. That ended our season of theatrical management. It also killed Mr. McCormick's ambition to become an actor, and partly killed mine. I still have hopes, however.

Well, after that I went to work — for a time. I went in to a big mill for three dollars per week. I was supposed to carry baskets full of coal from the basement to the top floor. The baskets were almost as big as myself. I reported for duty one fine summer morning at six o'clock. I carried up one basket ten minutes later. When I came back I asked the foreman if that was to be my daily toil. He replied "Yes." All I had to do was to put my hat on, and again I was free to participate in out-door sports. McCormick went to work — he got the fever for work a small boy always has when going to school — but his was a far more important position. He kept turning a crank which kept the mill going. If Mac went off to get a drink of water, the mill shut down until he returned. It used to shut down pretty often during his two days' connection with it. He got tired and gave up his work. He also had plenty of time that summer for out-door sports.

After that I went to work as the paper boy between New York and Paterson. I used to go up to New York every morning at four o'clock, and return at six with my papers. It wasn't very pleasant work, I assure you. But I had to do work of some sort, and I preferred that. It gave me a chance to "play ball" in the afternoon. Friends advised me to go to work and leave base ball alone. They predicted that it would ruin me. Friends are sometimes wrong. Never disappoint a boy, parents, if you wish him to be successful in this world. If he wishes to be a clergyman, do not change his mind. He may be a heart-broken, disappointed man in later years. There is everything in one picking out his vocation. It may be the stage, literature, art, the law, or something else. Give the boy a chance to select for himself. If he wishes to become a base ball player, encourage him to be an honest one. There is honor in every profession. 'Tis an honor to be an honest ball player. Be sure it's his vocation, first, then let him go ahead. You will never regret it.

Chapter III

In '73 I began to play in Paterson, N. J. McCormick came to me and said they were going to organize a base ball team, and asked me if I would join. I replied that I would be very happy to. We got together, and the next day the club was formed. Somebody wanted to name the club the Haymakers, but after a while I insisted that the Keystone was the best title. Mac agreed with me, and after due deliberation the club was called the Keystone. The captain of the club was William Purcell, who is now the captain of the Baltimore club. Purcell was a cranky sort of a boy at that time, but he could play great ball. He used to be all over the field, and kicked very strong when vigorous kicking was needed. McCormick, at that time, was about the same sort of a fellow that he is now. A great, big, soft-hearted boy. He was a good batter and very gritty. The great Nolan was the pitcher of our club, and a good pitcher he was. For several years we played together, and won game after game from the amateur clubs of Jersey. In 1876 Nolan quit us, and McCormick went in to pitch and I to catch. This is where we first got a reputation as the Keystone battery. It stuck to us for many years after. After the first season I was a valued member of the club. There was one cap in the nine, a fifteen-cent one, by the way, and I wanted it. Every boy in the nine did. Finally I said that if I didn't wear the cap I would not play in match games. Several of the club upheld me, and I wore the cap. The day I wore it was one of the happiest of my life. I felt that I was a "bigger man than old Grant," and strutted around the ball field like a game-cock.

Nolan, by the way, was a wonderful boy, too. Just now he is a great base ball authority in Paterson. He is on the police there, and he never misses a ball game that is played on his beat.

Our banner year was in 1876, when we beat all the Jersey clubs, and also several clubs from various parts of the country. We played a sort of co-operative game. Sometimes we got $1 for the day's work. Sometimes we got $4, but rarely more than $5. The only thing we were proud of in '76 was the defeat of the Stars, of Covington, Ky. They came our way and expected to slaughter us, but they didn't. We slaughtered them. They couldn't touch McCormick.

In the Stars at that time were Silver Flint, McSorley, Golden, Charley Foutz, later with the old St. Louis nine, and Andy Cummings. Silver Flint was at that time a tall, rawboned fellow, and was pretty innocent of the world and its ways. But it didn't take him very long to get initiated after he got into Chicago town. Chicago citizens have a knack of initiating a fellow pretty quickly after his arrival in town. Another crack club which we defeated that year was the Buckeyes, of Columbus. Everybody thought that they were invincible, until they met the old Keystones. In the Buckeyes at that time were Nolan, Barney, Ferran, Burke, Doescher, and Schaeffer. Burke was a splendid all-around player. He is at present in business at Albany, N. Y. Doescher was a member of the league umpiring staff last season. I regard him as being one of the best umpires in this country. He wasn't a great ball player, but he is a great umpire. George Schaeffer was afterwards in the Boston club. I believe that he is at present in Philadelphia. I saw him there the other day, and he looks just as young and handsome as he did in those days gone by. There was another good fellow in the nine, named Martin Nolan. He is now a successful lawyer in Columbus, O.

The great games of that season were played with the Mutuals, of Brooklyn. The Mutuals were, perhaps, the strongest base ball organization in New York. Well, we met them, and played a series of games for the championship. First one club would win a game then the other. In the club were Bobby Matthews, who is at it yet, Hicks, Nelson, and old Joe Start. There was a ball player for you. I regarded Joe Start as the most reliable man I ever saw cover the first bag, next to Anson. He saw his palmy days with the Mutuals, and later with the Providence club, when it was in the league. Not only could Joe Start bat well, but he could save the players more errors when covering the first bag than any man in the business. The games we had with the Mutuals finished the season in grand shape. It began to get cold, and finally the winter came. Like Othello, the ball player was without an occupation. I resolved to learn a trade. In the winter of 1877 I went into a factory to learn the silk weaver's trade. I stuck at it until the opening of the ball season. I was a crank on the game, and couldn't leave it alone if I wanted to. So I went at it again.

At the opening of the ball season that year I played several games with the Port Jervis team. I didn't care very much for the place, and jumped at an offer to go to the Buckeye club, with Jim McCormick for my pitcher. We had a great nine that year, and it was the first time that I really thought that I could play ball. Dorgan and I led off the batters. In the first game I made a base hit, and was so tickled that I started to steal second. I was thrown out, and the gang gave me the laugh. I didn't think that I was such a great ball player after that. I might have made the bag, too, but I had more confidence than I should have had. I thought that I could make it easy, but I couldn't.

Do you remember poor Chub Sullivan? What a big-hearted fellow he was. Chub was the first baseman of the team. He was a tall, handsome fellow, and one of the best dressed ball players I ever saw. He always wore fashionable clothes, and he was a fellow that could wear them, too. He died in Boston in 1882, and at the time, the Chicago club was in the city. They attended the funeral in a body. Chub Sullivan was a great ball player, and a grand good man in the bargain. He has been dead several years, yet his memory is kept green in the hearts of his friends. He was a man in every sense of the word. Among the other members of the club were George Streife, Burke, Harry Spence, who managed the Portland team last season and will manage the Hoosiers this year, and Charley Pabor, who is at present a member of the New Haven Police Force. They do say down in New Haven that Charley never missed a college game in the town. He almost went wild with joy when he saw the Yalensians beat the Boston league team at the opening of last season.

Well, we didn't get big salaries in those days, and a fellow was sometimes pretty lucky to get his salary. We didn't know the meaning of the words "advance money." Well, we didn't have a very prosperous season. The boys played good enough ball, but somehow or other they didn't seem to have the proper support from the patrons of the game. So on the nineteenth day of September the good old club disbanded. I looked about me, and didn't know just what I would do. I received a fine offer for me, at that time, to go with the Cincinnati club, and I accepted at once. I was more than glad to get in with such an array of talent as was in that club in '78. Just look at the names. There were Jim and Will White, who constituted the battery. The good old deacon could catch just as well in those days as he plays on a bag during the present time. Will White is in business in New Rochelle. Cal McVey — you all know Cal — left the base ball business, and is happy in the possession of a ranch out in California. Charley Jones — Bostonians remember Long Charley — was playing with the Metropolitans last season. In 1879 I was with the same club. The nine remained pretty much the same, with the exception of Ross Barnes, one of the best ball players I ever saw, who was an addition. In '79 we played pretty bad ball, and we were away down low in the league.

A little thing occurred this season which convinces me that circumstances can make or break a man's future. We started on our Eastern trip the latter part of May. We went first to Troy, thence to Syracuse, to Providence, ending in Boston. The team started out under the management of "Jim" White. Jim grew discouraged at the bad business, resigned while at Troy, and Cal McVey went into authority. We lost one game out of three at Troy, two out of three in Syracuse, three in Providence, and the first two in Boston. Dickerson, one of the club, was under the weather, and I was playing in pretty bad luck. After the second Boston game was finished, the record showed that out of the last twenty-one times at the bat I had reached first base but once, and that was by virtue of an error. McVey announced privately that night that he had telegraphed Jack Leary, who was then in Manchester, to come on the next day and play on the nine in the last game in Boston. He said that he hadn't made up his mind whether to lay off Kelly or Dickerson; the latter was still ill, but he did hit the ball occasionally; but he thought that I was the one to be relieved. With that impression McVey went to bed. Much to Cal's disappointment, Leary did not arrive in time for the game, and I was put in again to play right field. I knew what was going on, and I became so desperate that the ice was broken, and I succeeded in scattering my ill luck to the winds. I went to the bat five times, making two doubles, a triple, and a home run. Cal was delighted with my stick work that day. The team returned home, and we met the Chicagos. In the first game I was very lucky; I batted in every run made, and won the game for my club. At the end of the season I stood up among the leading batters. What might have been the result if Jack Leary appeared on the grounds in Boston? I would have been laid off, and returned to Paterson in disgrace. Perhaps I never would have had nerve enough to play in a league club again. That moves me to repeat the sacred thought:

> Great God, on what a slender thread
> Hang everlasting things.

Chapter IV

In the fall of that year I was with the Cincinnati-Buffalo combination which visited San Francisco. We remained their twelve weeks, played a good stiff game of ball, and came back with a pocketful of money. In the nine which visited 'Frisco were Jimmy Galvin, Clapp, John Reilley, Smith, now of the Pittsburgs, little Dave Force, whom we called the boy wonder, Jack Rowe, and Purcell. We arrived in 'Frisco, after a very pleasant journey, Oct. 5. We played the California nine at Oakland the next day, and beat them 5 to 0. The Hop Bitters team had arrived their about three weeks before us. The Californians thought they were the best ball team in the country. A game was arranged with this nine for the following Sunday. Expectations ran high, and their was great excitement, of course. There was more or less betting, the Hop Bitters team being the favorite with the sports. We whipped them in the first game by a score of 9 to 2, and there was tremendous excitement. Public opinion changed, and we were the greatest ball nine in the world. The next Sunday Chicago defeated us in the first game, and public opinion changed again, all of which convinces me that the public is very fickle, indeed. If you're on top, you're a great fellow. A man was never so great but that his place could be filled. The king is dead; long live the king. That's the way of the world, in base ball as well as in anything else. We played a series of games with the Chicago club, and each nine won three.

Did I ever tell how I signed with the Chicago club? Well, Anson became a bit interested in my playing. He asked me if I would like to become a member of the Chicago club, and I replied that nothing would please me better. Anson wired President Hurlburt, and he replied, "Get Kelly by all means." For two weeks Anson and I struggled before signing the contract. Anson wanted me for $100 less than my price. We met every day and talked the thing over. Anson was obstinate; so was I. Anson came into my room one day and said, "Well, Kel, are you going to sign?"

"No, sir," I replied, "not unless you give me the money I want. I am not at all particular to become a member of the Chicago nine, and unless I get the money I want, I would just as soon go somewhere else."

Anson looked at me, shrugged his shoulders, and said that I would be sorry by-and-by. I told him that I could stand it, if he could. As a matter of fact, it was the dream and ambition of my life to become a member of the Chicago club. I knew it meant lots of hard work, and I also knew that if I was a member of the club, and could play ball at all, Anson would be the one to give me a chance. He was always willing to push a young fellow ahead. He didn't know what professional jealousy meant. Well, I wasn't anxious that he should know that I wanted to go to Chicago. If he did, he would get me at his own price, just as sure as fate. So I remained indifferent. For several days I kept away from Anson. Finally, I was gathering my things and was about to start for home. Anson came up into my room. "Well, are you ready to sign, Kelly?"

"Quite ready, Mr. Anson, providing, of course, you pay me what I think is fair."

"Well, all right, my boy, you can have it. Put your name to the contract."

I did so, and in less than no time I was a member of the Chicago Base Ball Club.

Our club left San Francisco on the night of Dec. 19, and arrived at Council Bluffs Christmas night, in a blinding snow-storm. We were compelled to stop over, and went to the Ogden Hotel. You should have seen us when we entered the hotel. We were sights. The nine men wore beards that hadn't met with a razor for many, many days. We all wore flannel shirts, and when we registered the proprietor smiled all over, and welcomed the Cincinnati club to the Ogden. Then he invited us to a dance, which took place in the big dining-room. You should have seen those ten ball players march in to the dance-hall. Ten men with blue shirts, black ties and unclean faces. The ladies and gentlemen in the hall were frightened half to death. They had an idea that we were stage-coach robbers, or something of that sort. After they discovered that we were ball players, they forgot about our looks. They made us lions for the night. We danced there until 6 a.m. We arrived in

Cincinnati after a long trip, and on New Year's night I arrived home in Paterson.

What did I do?

Went straight to another dance, and was at it all night. I could dance in those days, because, you see, I never was bothered with "Charley Horse."

While at the dance I heard a conversation between McCormick's father and Purcell's father. Old McCormick was talking of a game of ball he saw the season before. He said: "Mr. Purcell, do yez know that the buoys gave your son great support all the past summer?"

"Indade, they did nothing of the sort," quoth Mr. Purcell, who seemed very mad.

"Why, of course they did," said McCormick, "and everybody knows it."

"Well, everybody doesn't know it, Mr. McCormick. No boys ever supported me boy. I've been a father to him and I've supported him for the past twenty years, and you bet yer sweet loife, Mike, that nobody can say anything to the contrary."

Chapter V

Two letters were received here at Hyde Park by me recently, one from Chicago, the other from a base ball enthusiast at Worcester. The Chicago man wanted me to tell what I "knew about base ball," the other asserting that people didn't care so much for the base ball part of it, but would like me to give impressions of some people I have met. I hardly think it would be interesting for me to give my impressions of the ball players I have met.

A man cannot always give his impressions of people he has met. Do you think so? It would be particularly hard to go through the list of ball players, and tell just what you think of them. I do not mean to cast any reflection upon the members of that profession. Not a bit of it. Tim Murnan — who can tell you more good stories to the square inch about ball players than any man in this country — once said to me: "Kel, ball players are as jealous of each other as two leading actresses in the same combination."

Several years' experience on the ball field convinces me that Tim was right.

Of course there is no exception without a rule. In some instances I've known players to speak in the highest terms of a man who was the star of the club he played in. Every club must have a star, just the same as a dramatic company must have a leading man.

In a small way I was a star myself last season. This was caused by the big sum of money paid for my release from Chicago. I didn't wish to have all the glory, because it was very inconvenient at times. Often on trips last season I was asked the question in hotels, "Which in Kelly?"

Sometimes Tate and sometimes Burdock would be pointed out as the man who was worth $10,000 in a base ball slave market.

But before going any further, it might be well to say that it's not well for any club to have a star player. Every man should receive fair, square treatment. The "star" never does. His words are quoted on and off the ball field, and if he makes the slightest mistake he is hissed and jeered.

As I remarked previously, the public is fickle. A man might make a wonderful play in one inning, and receive thunders of applause for so doing. In the next he might make an error, and the cheers would be changed to applause not so gratifying. A player doesn't always work for applause, or for the cheers of the grand stand. He can stand the cheers of the multitude all right, but the other applause is apt to rattle him, unless he is an old-timer.

Captain Anson, of the Chicago club, is one of the few men in the league that cannot be rattled under any circumstances. I've been on the ball fields with him, and heard five thousand people shouting, howling and hissing him, but he only smiled. He liked it. Yet he would come to the bat in the next inning, perhaps, and the hisses and howls would be changed to loud applause.

The crowd was fickle, and Anson won them over by displaying wonderful nerve. He is my ideal of what a player should be.

I was a bit afraid of Anson when I first met him. But after the first meeting we became fast friends, and our friendship has continued up to date, and I sincerely trust that it will ever be so.

Anson engaged me in 'Frisco in '79, and when I returned home I remained there just three weeks. I was ordered to report to Captain Anson at Chicago, April 1, 1880, and I did so. In the clubs I have played with before going to Chicago, I had a comparatively easy time. It wasn't necessary that one should train carefully, providing you played good ball. I expected a similar fate in Chicago, but how sadly was I disappointed.

Captain Anson met me there on a Sunday, and we had quite a long talk. He said that the next day he would take me around to see W. H. Hurlburt, then president of the Chicago club. Like many others who had never met Mr. Hurlburt, I stood in wholesome awe of him. A more thorough gentleman than he never lived. He was very kind to me at our first meeting, and told me just what the club expected. Our interview lasted but a few minutes, yet the impression remains with me still. Mr. Hurlburt lived just two years after he appeared first with the Chicago club. He was bothered all the while by heart disease, and his physicians advised him strongly against attending any of the games. But he was an ardent lover of the national game, and refused to heed their advice. He attended all the games up to '82, when he suddenly died, in April of that year. Although his death was expected, it caused a great deal of mourning throughout the country. Mr. Hurlburt was a man in every sense of the word. During the few years that I knew him I was with him very often. He was a big-hearted, honest, straightforward man. He did more to build up the national game than any one man in this country. He was a man of many resources, of great executive ability, and just as kindly and as soft-hearted as a child. God bless his memory. He was a noble man.

In the Chicago club of 1880 were Goldsmith and Corcoran, pitchers; Silver Flint, catcher; Quest, 2b; Williamson, 3b; Burns, s.s.; Dalrymple,l. f.; Gore, c. f.; Beals, substitute; Anson, 1b, and I played right field.

We were all pretty stout that first day of April, when we got into Chicago. I thought that perhaps we would do a little gymnasium work, and that's all. But how mistaken I was. It almost makes me shiver to think of it.

"How much do you weigh, Kel?" said George Gore to me one bright afternoon in the Chicago club-room.

"About one hundred and seventy," I replied; "but why do you ask?"

"Well, 'Ans' will be after you. You've got to come down about twenty pounds in the next few weeks."

I didn't quite realize what Gore meant at the time, but it wasn't very long before I did. Captain Anson ordered us to be ready for work on April 1, and we began to train for the summer. You haven't any idea what Anson meant by training. He meant training in every sense of the word. Directly after a light breakfast he would accompany us to the park, where the morning exercises would begin. We would walk a mile or so, to get limbered up, so to speak. Then Anson would lead the precession, and we would indulge in a fifteen-mile dog-trot.

He worked just as hard as the rest of us, and so we couldn't do any kicking. It wouldn't do any good, anyhow.

Then we would return to the hotel, have dinner, and rest for an hour or two. About two o'clock Anson would tell us to put our uniforms on. That meant a game of ball. It was a real game, too. No knocking up the ball and catching it was allowed. You would just have to get out in that field, and play as good ball as though there were five thousand spectators present at the game.

It was base ball all the time. When you hit a ball, even if it was gathered in by the pitcher, you would have to run to first base like a deer. If one didn't do it, the "old man" would be after him very strong. For a few days we were all broken up under his treatment. It was a bit heavy for us, you know. But after the first week we got used to it, and really enjoyed it. Anson himself would have as much fun on the field as a schoolboy let loose to play ball would have in an afternoon. He would grin when he struck out, and he would grin just the same if he caught "Goldie's" delivery for a base hit.

George Gore didn't like the training, and he suggested that we escape it for a couple of days, by feigning illness. There was some kind of sport going on down there, and we wanted very much to be present. We sent word down stairs in the morning that we were very ill, and wanted to be excused. Anson came up and looked at us.

"You fellows don't look very well," he said. "I guess a big dose of hot ginger won't do you any harm."

It was pretty rough on us, but we had to do the ginger up. Then Anson went off, whistling a merry tune. We were in bed — in lavender — when Anson returned. "Feel better?" he asked, and we replied, "No."

That meant another dose of ginger. Well, we stood it, thinking of the sport. Just as we were going to leave the hotel in a carriage, Anson came up and said: "Boys, I just felt a little ill myself, and thought I'd lay off this afternoon. But you both look healthy, and it braces me up. I guess the sport will get along without you both this afternoon. Come over to the park. We're going to have a little practice game over there."

We went with him. It was pretty hard to fool the old man.

When the season began, the result of Captain Anson's work was easily apparent. The boys played ball in great shape, and it was sure betting that we would win the championship. We did win it, too, although we had to make a pretty good fight for it.

That same nine played ball together for three years, and won the championship. In 1883 Boston wrested it from us. Never before was seen such batting and base running as those boys indulged in during the season of 1880. Why, it was scientific batting and base running from the start. Hurlburt had great confidence in the base-running qualities of the boys. I have heard Anson say, that at one of the exciting games there, he heard Hurlburt offer to wager that Kelly would score. Yet there were two men out, and I only made the first bag by a scratch. It was the best base-running nine that year I ever saw together. The men could run like deers, and we fooled most of the pitchers and catchers in the league that year.

Again, the batting of the boys was very scientific. It was the first time I ever heard of sacrifice hitting. If a man ever made a hit and got to first, the chances were ten to one that he would be sacrificed to third and then batted home. There were many other clubs who could outbat and outfield us in a game, yet we would win again and again under these circumstances.

The boys played great ball together, and they also did lots of kicking. I was a little behind the others in this respect on my first year, but I caught up and finished under the wire with them the next year.

Unless I am very much mistaken, I was the first one to introduce signs to the pitcher. I did it in the games I caught that year, and it caught on right away. Before the season was over, many a base runner was caught because of those signs. But after a year the custom spread. In two years about every pitcher and catcher in the league were using signs. How a little thing does spread. Why, at the present time you find boys, fifteen years old, playing ball and using all the signs like veterans. Verily, this is the age of progress.

We got quite a warm reception up in Worcester that year. When we reached the town there was quite a large gathering to see what we looked like. I heard one fellow say: "They look like murderers." He was half right. Seldom, indeed, would you see such a crowd of men. The members averaged six feet, and in weight about two hundred would be the limit. I wasn't near so heavy as that then, but have got nearer to it now.

Well, the fellows did some kicking on the field, and got the Worcester men pretty mad. There was lots of howling, and at one time it was feared that there would be a riot. But the Chicago club, each member with a bat over his shoulder, surrounded the umpire, and marched him off the field. Captain Anson led the precession with a bland smile upon his face, as much as if to say, "How tickled I am at the warmth of your reception." The Chicago club have on a good many occasions performed escort duty for umpires. We saved many a good fellow from being roughly handled by a crowd.

I remember an experience I had with Tommy Bond, when he was the crack pitcher of the Boston club. It was my first appearance in Boston with the Cincinnatis. I had quite a good reputation as a base runner, and Tom knew it.

"Wait till he tries to steal a bag on me this afternoon," he said in the

United States Hotel to McVey. "I'll kill him, sure, before he reaches the base."

I heard this, and made up my mind that Tommy would have lots of killing to do. Well, he hadn't. I made the first base once, in a scratch hit out of five times at the bat.

"You're going to steal it, are you?" said Tommy, and I replied that "I was."

Well, I was pretty confident, and started down for that bag like a streak of lightning. But Snyder was "on," and the ball got there before I did. The result was that White, McVey, Bond, and all the boys gave me the grand laugh.

I felt pretty bad that night, and resolved to get even the next day. This time I kept things to myself. I made three base hits off Bond, and stole three bases. One of these was from second to third, while Snyder was returning the ball to Bond. The laugh that night was all on Bond, but he stood it cheerfully, and said that "Kelly deserved to get there, because he had nerve enough to take the chances."

Chapter VI

The Chicago club always had to play a pretty stiff game of ball, to win from the other league clubs. There was always more or less feeling against the nine in various quarters, probable because they were such great kickers at times. However, the boys didn't mind this very much; in fact they enjoyed it. It spurred them on, sometimes, to play great ball. I think the three most exciting games of ball I ever played in, were against the Providence team, at Chicago, in 1882. The games practically settled which nine was to wave the championship pennant. The Providence club came to Chicago, four games ahead of the White Stocking nine. George and Harry Wright were two of the first members of the club that I met near the dressing-room. Harry was the manager of the Providence club then, and George was the short-stop. The latter was a great short-stop. He picked up a ball with great neatness and dexterity. He was a good, safe thrower, and seldom, indeed, did he make a mistake. A very gentlemanly fellow both on and off the ball field, he had a good many friends, both in and out of the base ball profession. He is now in business in Boston with Henry Ditson, a bright young fellow, who is a great lover of lawn tennis.

Both the Wrights were confident that Chicago would drop three straight games to the Providence boys, and that they would win the championship. I wanted to bet Harry a new hat, but he wouldn't bet. The first game was the most hotly contested game of ball I ever played in. Every point was fought, and each man exerted every effort to have his side win. We, perhaps, had a little the best of it, in view of the fact that we were at home, and were sure to get the encouragement of the thousands of spectators who witnessed the game. The score in the last inning was four to three in favor of the Providence club. There was one man out when I scratched a hit. I got on first and was about to make an attempt to steal second, when Burns, who followed me, hit a hot grounder to George Wright. There was one player out, and if George ever got the ball to second it meant a double play, and that would settle the game. Instead of fielding the ball to the second baseman, he started for the bag himself. I never ran so hard in my life. I reached the bag a second before George, and then like a flash, he raised his arm to send the ball to the first base, to cut off Burns. Somehow or other an accident occurred at that moment. My arm went up in the air, and it caught George on the shoulder. The result was, that when the ball left George's hand it went away over into the grand stand. I scored first, and Burns followed me a moment later. The cheers from a thousand enthusiastic spectators, proved that the Chicago club had won the first great game. The next two were afterwards won by us, and in the ten games that followed with other clubs, Providence won but two.

Harry Wright was the maddest man in Chicago when the series had finished, and he claimed that were it not for "Kelly and his infernal tricks," the Providence club would have won the series and the championship. He swore that he would have revenge in the future. I saw him, and had quite a talk with him. I said, "Mr. Wright, I have played ball for a number of years; I will do everything in the world to win a championship game of ball. That is what I am paid for. But during all the time I have played ball, I never hurt a player. I never spiked a man, never knocked a man down. I play ball to win, and if I have to employ a few subterfuges to win I cannot help it. I wouldn't wilfully hurt George Wright, or any man in your club. But self-preservation is the law of nature. When I saw George raise his arm, I knew that if something didn't occur we would be defeated. I didn't think of George nor myself. I simply thought of the Chicago club." Harry was smiling before I finished, and he was willing to forgive me. Instead of having revenge, he has been a good friend of mine since that time.

The Chicago club had considered fun at my expense, early in this season, "82. It seems that something or other I did in Boston the previous season — I did so many things to displease Bostonians in those days that I cannot remember just what it was — had aroused the ire of the Boston press. The papers went for me hot, and all sorts of threatening things were said. Of course all the boys had the papers, and they showed them to me day after day. Finally it looked as though I would be mobbed if I went to Boston. The boys worked on me so that I got ill, and wanted to be excused from making the trip. But Anson refused to accept the excuse. Williamson came to me one day, and advised me to cut my hair off. He thought that if I did, that I wouldn't be recognized in Boston. I went to the barber's, and had all the hair taken off, the barber using a sort of horse-clipping machine. The next day it was Silver Flint's turn. He advised me to have the moustache shaved off. He claimed that if this was done, I would escape the vigilance of the Boston Judge Lynch party. Off came the moustache; it was Burns' turn next. He advised me to wear different clothes, and I took his advise. I went to Boston disguised like the French detectives we read about. I was the most disappointed man in Boston. There wasn't any outbreak; in fact, I was treated in a very kindly manner, far better, in fact, than I deserved. The boys all had the laugh on me. My hair was gone, and so was that "beautiful moustache," as Flint said. I was more than willing that they should do all the laughing. This experience convinced me that although newspapers can do a good deal for good or evil, they cannot start a riot.

Chapter VII

A great deal of responsibility rests upon the shoulders of a captain in a professional ball club. He is in a measure responsible for a man off as well as on the field. If a player is not in good condition to play a good, strong game, the captain is the one to be censured by the management. If the captain in return censures the player, by fining him, the chances are that he has made an enemy. The result is, that if four or five men are fined, the captain soon discovers that life to him is somewhat of a burden. He can see that the men are not playing good ball, but he cannot openly accuse them of this. If he levies another fine, there is going to be another row.

The captain of a ball club has to be a man of considerable discretion. He is always compelled to have a level head and an even temper. He must know just the moment to kick at a decision of an umpire; he must know the moment to give the umpire what the small boy calls "taffy." He must always encourage his players; never discourage them, even if half a dozen strike out every time they come to the bat. He must listen to their grievances, and sympathize with them in their misfortune. He must tell them that they are great players, and that base ball couldn't get along without them. He must have the confidence of the management, or he cannot be a success. It may seem pleasant and profitable to be the captain of a nine, but it isn't. I had quite enough of it for one season, thank you. In the future I am more than contented to go out into the field and just "play ball" for a pastime.

In my year's experience as a captain, I never fined a player. Perhaps I may have had good cause to in one or two instances, but I didn't. What good would it do if I did? It would not improve the playing of the men any, nor would it help me in the end. Trouble enough will come to a captain without his going in search of it. When I was a boy, playing ball, it was the ambition of my life to wear a white belt, on which was to be marked in vermilion letters "captain." I've grown older since. Now, I would rather see the other fellow wear the white belt, on which was inscribed the letters of vermilion hue.

Who is the greatest captain in the league? Capt. A. C. Anson, of the Chicago club! He is, without doubt, the most successful captain in the league. I say this without the least desire to injure any of the other gentlemen who fill the same position in other clubs.

I do not mean that Anson is the only good captain in the country. Not by any means. We have had and have some wonderfully clever men playing on the field, who have made great reputations in this position.

John M. Ward, to my mind, was a great captain. He could see the fine points in a game as quick as any man who stepped on a ball field. Quick and alert, he was always ready to make a good, strong fight for his side. Ward knows as much, if not a little more, about the rules of base ball, than any man in the country. He is a scholarly gentleman, a good fellow, and a great ball player. Ward's great hobby is the brotherhood; and, while some may question its entire success, there isn't any doubt that were it not for Ward's headwork and persistency, no such organization would be in existence. There are some managers who do not believe in the brotherhood, and assert that it will never amount to anything. Well, perhaps it won't. Yet with Ward at its head, you can depend upon it the brotherhood is a strong factor in the national game. It can exert a wonderful power for good or evil. I hope it will be for good.

"Buck," or William Ewing, of the New Yorks, is another good captain. "Buck" may not have such a good base ball head as Ward, but he has hustling qualities which generally land him among the winners. "Buck" is a splendid fellow personally, and is one of the best-natured men in the profession. In some quarters he is looked upon as a kicker. But he is a good-natured kicker, whose little kicks never leave a sting behind.

Arthur Irwin is a captain who has come strongly to the front in the past few years. He is in many respects a good captain. Were it not for ill health at times, he would be great. Irwin is quiet and gentlemanly on the ball field, but he can stick out as long as any other man, when occasion requires. He has handled his men in great shape, and should be given lots of credit for the fine showing made by his nine. Irwin has brought the "Phillies" to the front so rapidly that it wouldn't surprise me a bit to see him land them number one one of these days.

In regard to the great captains of the country, I would like to say a word about John Morrill, of the Boston nine.

During the winter, and more particularly during my last visit to Boston, I heard in certain quarters that Morrill and Kelly were not good friends. This statement is false in every particular. Morrill and I are, and always have been, the very best of friends. I did not know Morrill very well until I joined the Boston club. I found him a pleasant, affable gentleman, and I do not think a man ever played ball in the Boston nine who doesn't say the same thing. It was also said that there was rivalry between Morrill and Kelly; it was hitting that Morrill wanted to be manager and captain, and that Kelly wanted the same positions. This is also silly and false. From the day that I was appointed captain of the Boston club, John Morrill did everything in his power to make my *regime* a success. I wasn't any more anxious then to be captain than I am now. But I had to take that which was thrust upon me. John Morrill knows this as well as I do. If Morrill was jealous, then he had a peculiar way of showing it. He exerted himself in every conceivable manner to help me out. He did so many times, and I would indeed be ungrateful if I did not fully appreciate his worth, both as a man and as a ball player.

There are few players in this country who are as well posted on the rules of base ball as John Morrill. He doesn't have a great deal to say, perhaps, but he keeps up an awful thinking all the time. As a baseman he has but one superior, to my mind, and that one is A. C. Anson. Morrill is a careful man, and saves the Boston club a good many dollars in the course of a year, as a manager. He is worth a load of money to the Boston management, and I think the three magnates appreciate his worth. If they don't, they make a very great mistake. Morrill is a good manager, and a first-class captain. He handles his men in good shape, and treats one and all justly and honestly.

Now I have all these men in mind, when I say that A. C. Anson is the best field captain we have in this country. I worked under him for several years, and know of just what stuff he is made. Anson was born in Iowa, and thirty-five years ago. He's a giant, standing six feet two inches tall, and weighing, when in good condition, just about two hundred and twenty pounds. His long connection with the Chicago club has made him famous in every city in this country.

He made his first trial at base ball in 1871, and was a success from the start. He's been at it ever since. Since coming into the league, he has made the best record of any man at batting. He has been first three times; second, three times; fourth, twice; fifth, twice, and sixth once. Isn't that a record for a man to feel proud of? He has had the championship in his city for a greater number of years than all the others combined. Isn't this a record to be proud of?

Why is it that Anson has been so successful? It's a comparatively easy matter to answer the question. He enthuses his followers. He doesn't demand it, but does ask politely that every man who steps on a field shall play ball from beginning to end. If his club is seven runs ahead in the last inning, he's going to have his men play as hard as if they were just seven behind. Anson has no favorites. He won't have any in his club. He treats all men alike. I was as near to him as any man who ever played ball in the White Stocking nine. Yet never did he show it, on or off the field. He treated me like the rest, never better, and once and a while a bit worse. When it was the latter, I thoroughly deserved it.

Anson is the easiest captain in the league to get along with, if you mind your own business,— the hardest, if you won't. He thoroughly believes in discipline.

Sometimes he is apt to be harsh, but when he is it is with a man whom the other players think is the white-headed boy. He watches every point in the game. Nothing escapes him. He is working all the time for success, and, as a result, his men are bound to do the same thing. He is good-natured, too, even when he is making a great fight. There was supposed to be some feeling between Anson and myself, but it isn't so. There never was and never will be.

I remember a little incident that occurred last summer, which tickled him so that he was good-natured for days afterwards. I made a base hit, and I think there was only one out. I stole second, and the next batter bunted the ball to Williamson, and the latter picked it up and sent it to Anson. We needed the run badly, and I was also very tired in the bargain. So I started to run to third, but cut across the diamond in my haste, and making a long slide, reached the home plate before the ball arrived. Anson was very mad, or appeared to be, but I could see that he was grinning. He couldn't help it. He was reminded of old times. He rushed up to Phil Powers and made a great kick. Powers declared me out, but, as a matter of fact, I wasn't. He didn't know whether I had touched third bag or not. Anson chuckled grimly, and returned to the first bag. After the game he said:

"Well, Kel, you didn't get there after all, did you? I'm surprised that you would attempt anything so dishonest."

"So am I," I replied, "but were it not for you and Chicago, I would never try things of that sort. When I did it first you thought it was great. It tickled you immensely. You can't go back on what you have said in the past, can you?"

"Well, it's just here, Kel. It was all right in Chicago, but times have changed since then. I'm watching you all the time when we're playing, Kel, and I'm willing to say that you keep me thinking. But, old man, do you know what I felt when you stole across the diamond? I felt like shouting, 'Hurry up, Kel, or Powers will be on.'"

Anson took more long chances to win a game of ball than any other captain I ever saw. I have seen him win a game under very peculiar circumstances.

We were playing against the New Yorks. It was in the last inning, and the game was five to five. McCormick was pitching and I was catching. McCormick had pitched in two or three games that week with a pretty sore arm. He was pretty tired in the last inning, and Anson was the first to notice it. The umpire called a good ball a strike, and Anson objected. To his mind, he said, it should have been a ball. He had a ten-minute argument, and getting near me, gave the tip that I should hurt my finger. The next ball pitched did that. I had to go in the dressing-room, and it was fully ten minutes before I could show up. In the meantime Fred Pfeffer had been hurt by a pitched ball in the practising, and as a result, there was almost half an hour's delay. Mac braced up and felt pretty good again. He pitched a great inning, and then we made one run in the next. We had won the game. If McCormick had not got that rest, we would have been slaughtered.

On another occasion we were two runs behind the Detroits. A man was on second, and a base hit was sent into the field, which would have allowed him to score. But he didn't. He tripped when he reached third, and got mixed up with the bag. That is just what Anson wanted him to do. Then the man on first stole second, and a base hit brought in two runs. A couple of sacrifice hits just won that game.

He has tried and invented more schemes to win games than any player living. He will advise his men to steal bases, and will encourage them if they fail.

"Never mind, old fellow," he will say, "you made a great bluff at it. You'll get it the next time, you bet."

He never discourages a player, and when a young man comes into the club, he treats him like a younger son until the young man gets fresh, and then is sat down on very, very hard. As a result, the players are always working hard to win the love of the old man. When they make a brilliant play, he is the first one to come forward and say something about it. When a poor play is made does he kick? Not at all. He simply tells the man who makes the error that mistakes will happen, but cautions him to try and be a little more careful.

There isn't any doubt about his standing, at all. He is the greatest captain in the league. He plays just as hard to win exhibition games from minor clubs as he does to win the league championship games. I talked with Walt Williams, the well-known "monopole" agent in the Hoffman House, at the close of the season of '87. Mr. Williams is a Chicago man, and knows Anson very well.

He said, "Well, Kel, Anson couldn't win this year, could he? He cannot win with an indifferent nine."

"That's so," I replied, "but he can make nine poor players go on the field and make them play a stiffer game of ball than any man living."

Anson, I really believe, can take nine raw men who never saw a ball game, and in two months he will make ball players of them. He is a good fellow, a staunch friend, and I hope he will be for many years to come, what he is today, the greatest base ball captain in this country.

Chapter VIII

There is lots of luck about base ball. There isn't any doubt about that. This factor — for it is a factor — enters largely into the game. Sometimes we see the giant club of the league fall before the weakest clubs. Yet the very next day the tables will be turned. This is due to several causes. For instance, a club is apt to be in great condition as a whole one day, the next some one or two men are apt to be badly broken up. A base ball player is a tough, hardy individual as a rule, but he cannot stand any more than two ordinary horses, although he is generally supposed to.

A player cannot offer illness as a plea if he plays a weak game of ball. If he does, nobody will believe him. He must play a good, strong game, day after day, be he healthy or ill. Now, if one man is badly broken up, the result is that the whole club soon becomes demoralized. Six men cannot win a game, seven cannot, eight cannot, neither can nine, sometimes. I have known instances when it was absolutely necessary for the umpire to move his trunk, so to speak, into the club he works for, and help his players to win a victory. It requires ten good, healthy men to win a game of this sort. But as a rule, nine men are quite sufficient. But they must be healthy, and in good condition, or they cannot win, even if luck is with them. What I want to say is this: To be successful, and win games, there must be nine men in a club who are working and striving shoulder to shoulder, on a steady march to victory. There must be no dissensions, no petty jealousies, no malice, no spite of any sort. The men must be good friends, and have things so arranged that one man stands perfectly willing to help another. That's just the secret of the success of the Chicago club. Captain Anson has his players well in hand. He makes them companionable, treats one man no better than another, and always tries to make them very best of friends.

One reason for the failure of other clubs, is the ill feeling in the ranks. Base ball players sometimes are as difficult to handle as actors. One player discovers another receives a few dollars more salary than he receives. He thinks he is far more valuable to the club, and he goes to the manager and tells him what he thinks. The manager tries to pacify him, but doesn't succeed. The player begins to be jealous, then he makes up his mind to let the club "hustle for itself." He will play for himself, and play for a record. Another player may have another slight grievance, and he also goes to the manager. The latter does the best he can, but he cannot perform impossible things; the result is, there is another dissenting element in the club; there is another record player. It's little things of this sort which makes the "grand stand player." They make impossible catchers, and when they get the ball they roll all over the field.

Is it necessary to do this latter feat?

Well, sometimes it is, and sometimes it isn't.

As a rule, it is done just to win the applause of the grand stand. I have no regard for such players. Possibly because I cannot perform the "feat" myself. It's a pretty difficult matter for me to catch a high fly, anyway. I never practised the rolling on the ground part of it. If I did, I have an idea that I would drop the ball, and then the "grand stand" would make it very warm for me for a few moments.

You can depend upon it, that it takes just nine healthy, peaceable men, who are playing together, for each other and for the good of the club they work for, to win a game of ball.

I have seen clubs in that condition. When the Chicago club came to Boston, at near the close of the season of 1883, we found the Bostons in this condition. The home club was playing a faultless game. They were in great trim. They were batting well, playing a great fielding game, ran bases in good shape, and had a get-there air of confidence which would demoralize almost any club. On the other hand, the Chicagos were pretty well broken up. "Silver" Flint had a broken finger, and couldn't catch. I was also troubled with a broken finger, and every time I caught a ball it seemed as though my right hand would drop off. Neither Corcoran nor Goldsmith were in good condition, and they didn't pitch anywhere near the game they were capable of doing. Anson went in to catch, and so did Williamson. When we came to Boston, we had only ten games to play: four in Boston, three in

Providence, and three in New York. We led the league by four games. We knew that if we finished in Boston all right, that we would make a strong fight for the pennant. Anson never encouraged the boys so in his life. But we had a good nine, in great condition, to oppose us, and we couldn't do impossible things. The Boston nine was made up of Whitney and Buffinton, pitchers; Hines and Hackett, catchers; Morrill, Burdock and Sutton, on the bases; Wise, short-stop; while Hornung, Smith and Radford were in the right field.

What great excitement there was on the South End grounds those closing days. How the boys did guy Anson, and I came in for my share of it. I never thought then that I would at a future time be a member of the nine I was fighting against, tooth and nail.

It was a good nine, and the games were won for several reasons: one, because the Chicagos were pretty well broken up; the wonderful pitching of big Jim Whitney and Buffinton; and the most important reason of all, because the Bostons played better ball and made more runs. Guess that's the best way out of it. You all know how great the excitement was in Boston, at the time. Boston deserved the honor. The boys won that pennant fairly and squarely. We accepted defeat like philosophers, and made up our minds to even things up at some future day. Well, the four games we lost at Boston, demoralized us. We couldn't do anything with New York or Providence, and that settled it.

I had a very curious experience with a Boston gambler at that time, which is worth recalling now. This fellow came to me in the corridor of the United States Hotel the night after the first game.

"Kelly," he said, "I have it on pretty good authority that Chicago is going to throw the championship to Boston this year. Is it so?"

I looked at him for a moment, and thought perhaps that he was joking. I sized him up, and then said to him:

"You had better ask Anson. He knows more about it than I do."

"Look here, Kelly," the fellow replied, "what Anson knows in regard to this affair, doesn't matter. You fellows can win it, if you want to. There isn't any doubt about that, in my mind. Now, I'm in this thing to make money, and I am willing to help you do the same. I understand that you are to catch in the coming games. If you will promise me that the Bostons will win, I will give you $2,500. You can fix the pitchers."

The proposition stunned me for a moment. Anson was in the office. I called him over, and told him what the man had said. He just stood there like a dummy, but looked as though he would like to be present somewhere else. I thought Anson would get mad, but he didn't. He said, "My friend, you cannot buy the Chicago club. There isn't money enough in Boston for that. Now, I will give you a straight tip. If we can win, we are going to. We're going to make the great fight of our lives. I heard, on the very best authority, tonight, that the Bostons were going to do the same thing. One thing I will admit. This week settles whether it will be Boston and Chicago, or Chicago and Boston. Good-night, sir. I'll play you a game of billiards, Kel."

The man looked as though he wished he were dead.

A great many people in this lovely country of ours, have an idea that the gamblers run base ball, and that a player can easily be bought, one way or the other. This is the most absurd idea imaginable. To be sure, there is more or less betting in every game which attracts sporting men. You will find this the ease, from the third-class races at Clifton to the swell races of the Country Club. But on one thing I will risk everything I have in the world: there is no dishonesty about base ball.

The games are played for all they are worth; and of the many players at present in the league, I am sure there is not one dishonest one. There may have been a few in the past. Let us thank God that there are none in the present, and hope that there won't be in the future.

The various base ball managers throughout the country pay a large sum of money annually to their players. They pay enough for them to be honest. They are honest. Any time you ever hear a man speak about base ball, and say that it is a dishonest game, you can set him down as being either a fool or an idiot.

This is gospel truth.

Before proceeding any further, I want to tell you a little incident which occurred coming from New York to Washington, some time since. I sat with a friend, a few seats in the rear of a young man who was made up as a dude. A little five-year-old boy sat with his mother on the opposite side of the pullman.

"What does you call him, mamma?"

"That, my child, is a young man."

"Isn't dat what you call a dude, mamma?"

"Hush, my child; yes, that's a dude."

"So, 'ees a dude, mamma? But, mamma, who made him?"

"Hush, hush, my child; God made him."

"Oh! yes. Mamma, God likes to have fun, sometimes, doesn't he?"

This isn't base ball, but, like what I've said about the men who wager money on ball games, it's gospel truth. Marshal P. Wilder has already claimed this story as his.

Chapter IX

I shall not attempt to tell of how games were won season after season. Some day, perhaps, I shall. Even if I felt disposed to do so now, it would require a book almost three times the size of the one I am presenting to the public. Then the championship games are of such a recent date, that many of you know almost as much about them as the author of this book.

I have several times referred to the Boston club, and to the Modern Athens. While a member of the Chicago club, I always held a high opinion of the Hub, and of the boys who played ball in its club.

It was a strange fact, but nevertheless a true one, that Boston always played a stronger game against Chicago than any club in this country. I have, on a number of occasions, tried to find a satisfactory meaning for this, but after considerable thought, finally arrived at several conclusions.

To begin with, there was always great rivalry between the two clubs. Boston might play a miserable game in Boston, with some of the weakest clubs in the league. The next week, or the next day, perhaps, Chicago would come along and expect to win an easy series of victories. Well, the Chicago club would have to fight every inch of the game to win, if they did win.

Some of the most exciting games I ever participated in were played in Boston. Many and many a time have the Boston boys been all broken up before the arrival of the Chicago nine, but somehow or other they would brace up sufficiently to give Anson and his men a very warm welcome, indeed.

It was the same in Chicago. The White Stockings might be playing bad ball until Boston would arrive. Then they would go on the field and play a perfect game. Why, it would be almost impossible to get a ball by that infield, even if it was shot forth from the mouth of a cannon.

I have another reason for the fine play between these two clubs. You see, the people who go to the ball grounds enter into the spirit of the game. They make up their minds to see some fun when Boston and Chicago come together. Well, they generally see it. They expect and want lots of kicking. They generally get it, some time or other before the game closes. They want to do lots of shouting, and they have their way. They encourage the players, especially the home players, at every possible opportunity. A play that wouldn't receive any attention with another club, is greeted with hearty cheers if the play is against Chicago.

What is the result?

The men play better ball on both sides. The home players are on the *qui vive*, and play all the ball they know how. The visiting players get mad, because they have an idea that they should get a little of the applause. Well, they just grit their teeth, and swear under their breaths that they are going to win the game, anyhow. So, you see, it's a pretty even thing, any way you look at it. As a result, the public see some wonderfully good games of ball.

I have talked with John Morrill several times about this. He holds a similar opinion to mine. He says Boston always plays a better game against Chicago than against any other city. On the other hand, I know that Chicago, even when broken up, will play a strong game with Boston. For one, I am very glad that there is such a strong rivalry between the two cities. It adds interest to the games, and makes them as exciting to the men on the field as to the spectators.

I always had a regard for Boston, and the people who saw the games in the Hub. This was on account of the treatment I always received at the South End grounds. Sometimes, perhaps, I would be "guyed" as strongly even as Anson, but, as a rule, I always received the very best treatment. This is saying a great deal, considering the fact that I was a member of a visiting club, and had the reputation of being a tricky man on the field. How a Boston audience would shout and roar, with mingled feelings of anger and joy, when I would cut the third bag on my way home. It almost reminded one of hundreds of insane people let loose. Yet, if I made a good play in the next inning, it would be greeted with shouts of honest applause. In that respect, Boston leads the base ball cities of the country. The spectators are more fair minded, and will applaud the visiting players heartier than in any other city in this country. I've been to them all, and know just what I'm talking about. It's a great city. It's a great base ball city. I am more than proud to be a member of the Boston nine. It makes me happy to feel that I'm Kelly of Boston, instead of Kelly of somewhere else.

I never imagined, however, that I would be a member of the Boston nine. Yet, at the close of the season of 1886, I had some trouble with the Chicago management. I felt that Messrs. Spaulding & Co. had not treated me fairly. I told President Spaulding as much when the season closed. He smiled, and regarded it as a Kelly joke. He said he guessed when the next season came around he would have things so arranged that I would be a member of the Chicago club. I said to him:

"President Spaulding, at the close of the season I'm going up to Hyde Park, in New York, for the winter. My brother-in-law has a farm there. If I'm not a member of some other club next season, you will find that farming is good enough for me during the summer. I will not play again in the Chicago club, under any circumstances, and don't you forget it."

Well, I meant just what I said. After leaving Mr. Spaulding, almost the first man I met was Nat Goodwin, the Boston actor. Nat and I were always great friends, and had been for several years. He was playing in Chicago at the time. He invited me around to his rooms in the Palmer House. Naturally enough, I told him of the conversation I had just had with Mr. Spaulding. Goodwin heard it all, and then said:

"Kel, don't play in Chicago. You stick to what you said."

"But where would be the best city for me to play?" I inquired.

"The best city in the country for you to play ball, Kel, is in Boston. You hang out, and I will make an even bet that you will be a member of the Boston club next season."

We had quite a long conversation, and I promised Goodwin that if it could be arranged, I would gladly go to Boston the next season. I think that when Nat and his manager, George Floyd, reached Boston, they saw the Boston managers, and told them what I had said. I met Goodwin in New York in November, I think it was, and he told me it was all right. He said I would be in Boston next year, if money would buy my release. I thought it was all right then, because I didn't have any idea that so much money would be paid for the release of a player as was paid for mine.

About the 1st of December, '86, I wrote from Hyde Park to Mr. Spaulding. The newspapers had been saying some pretty hard things about me, and one or two of them printed interviews with Spaulding, in which he said a number of things which were more than unfair. In this letter, I told him that I would not play in Chicago; that I never had been under any obligations to the club, as I had always worked hard for what I got. I wrote again, the latter part of the month, and in return I received a letter from President Spaulding, in which he denied several interviews alleged to have come from him.

For the time being, that ended our correspondence.

Without any knowledge on my part, Mr. Billings went to work on the Boston end, and began making overtures to Mr. Spaulding. The latter refused the first offer of $5,000 for my release. Then Mr. Billings raised the amount to an even $9,000. Mr. Spaulding replied that if he would make it $10,000, and wait until the middle of March, to give him a chance to interview the directors, he thought it would be all right. But Mr. Billings wasn't waiting. He wrote Mr. Spaulding that he would give $10,000 for Kelly's release, but that the offer might be accepted at once. This offer caught Spaulding, and he didn't delay any in replying, "All right."

Armed with Mr. Spaulding's letter, Mr. Billings, accompanied by W. D. Sullivan, then the sporting editor of the Boston *Globe*, came to Poughkeepsie, N. Y., on Feb. 14, 1887. I drove over from Hyde Park, and met them at the Nelson House. I had just about one hour's talk with Mr. Billings. When he left the hotel, he had my name signed to a contract. I was a member of the Boston club, and I haven't had any reason to regret my choice. At that time I had an idea that I would rather play on the New York nine. In fact, I was offered $7,750 to get my release from Chicago, and a promise of $5,500 salary in the bargain.

Well, Spaulding wouldn't allow me to go to New York, anyhow, and, on the whole, I thank him for it. It would be impossible for a man to receive better treatment than was accorded me in Boston.

A few days after all the arrangements were made, I received a characteristic letter from Mr. Spaulding. It is certainly worth a place in this book, although he does rub it in to me more than he should. Mr. Spaulding evidently forgot that I always worked for the interest of the Chicago club. I played ball for the nine when so ill, that to move about caused the greatest suffering. But never mind that; I'm away from the club. It won't kill either of us. As Mr. Spaulding says, somebody will always spring up, and take our places when we disappear. That's gospel truth. The Chicago club got along nicely without me last year, and I got along without Chicago. But enough; here is his letter:—

Chicago, Feb. 19, 1887.
M. J. Kelly, Hyde Park, N. Y.

Dear Sir:—I am in receipt of your picture, in costume and batting position, and the same has been handed to our engraver, with instructions to get out as good a cut as possible for the forthcoming Guide.

I congratulate you on the magnificent salary that I understand you will receive from the Boston club next season, and I hope you will not disappoint them, but will make yourself not only worthy of the amount that you will receive from them, but also of the very large bonus that they have paid the Chicago club for your release. I am just in receipt of a letter from Mr. Billings, from which I quote as follows:

"Kelly did not say a word against you; said the Chicago club was a good one to get money of, when wanted. Anson worked him pretty hard sometimes, when not in condition, and there is where the trouble lies, I think."

I am very glad to know that you have no personal feeling towards me, for I certainly have none towards you, and I do not believe you can truthfully say that either myself or the Chicago club have taken any advantage of you, but have always treated you right and fair. I have placed no credence in the rumors and alleged interviews, that have been published in the New York papers, from time to time, knowing, from my own experience, how these interviews are manufactured. As you will, no doubt, be captain of the Boston nine, you will find it necessary, or at least it will be advisable, to set examples to your men in the way of habits and deportment, that will be an incentive for them to follow....

Wishing you every prosperity and success in your new position, I am,

Yours truly,
G. SPAULDING.

Chapter X

It was at near the close of the season of 1886, that I first shook hands with a President of the United States. We were playing off three of the last games with the Washingtons. Captain Anson wanted very much to meet the President. He said that "President Cleveland was a mascot," and he wanted to grasp his hand. He had the same strong desire to shake Cleveland's hand as "Old Sport," in "A Rag Baby," has to grasp the hand of the man that shook hands with John L. Sullivan. Well, Anson hunted up all over the town, and finally discovered the congressman from one of the Chicago districts. He said he would try and fix things so that we would meet the President the next day.

He came, according to agreement, and said the President would like to meet us. Captain Anson got us together, and, headed by the congressman, we marched to the White House. It was a good-looking crowd of men that marched behind Captain Anson that day. There was George Gore, who shook the Chicago dust from his base ball shoes, and who now plays with the New Yorks. McCormick, whom I regard with almost brotherly affection, and who twirls the sphere for Pittsburg now. Burns and Dalrymple were also present. There wasn't a man in the crowd who wasn't almost six feet in height, and they were all in lovely condition. Their hands were as hard as iron. Dan Lamont met us, and, escorted by him, we marched to the room where the President was.

President Cleveland wore a Prince Albert coat, tightly buttoned, and he looked much stouter than the photographs we had seen of him led us to believe. While Lamont was talking to him, Captain Anson was puzzling his brain for a few words to say, suitable for the occasion. But the President didn't give him or any of us a chance for formal words. He was as affable and as courteous as it was possible for a man to be.

"President Cleveland, this is Captain Anson, of the Chicago Base Ball Club," said Colonel Lamont.

"I'm happy to meet you, Captain Anson. You have the champion ball club, I believe."

Anson gripped his hand. Then I was the second man to be introduced. The President's hand was fat and soft. I squeezed it so hard that the President winced. Then George Gore did the same. Burns gave the President another warm grip, and Dalrymple did likewise. When it came to McCormick, the President's good right hand was almost doubled up. McCormick shook his hand warmly; so warmly, indeed, that President Cleveland looked glad and happy when it was all over. He would rather shake hands with one thousand people than two ball nines, after that day. He conversed with us for a good half hour. He spoke of early days in Buffalo, when he used to be a great admirer of base ball, and how, when young, he used to toss the ball himself, occasionally. He said laughingly, that he was so stout then that he didn't think that there was a fat man's nine in the country which would care to make him a member. The President didn't shake hands again when we parted. He remembered the grip of a few minutes before. He wished us all good luck and prosperity. He impressed me as being a charming, courteous gentleman, who has considerable backbone, and democratic enough to be a Democratic President of our glorious country.

Chapter XI

I shall never forget the opening game of the season in Boston, May 9, 1887. It was the most memorable night in my life. We played the opening game with Philadelphia, and were defeated. After the game, John Graham, a well-known member of the Boston Lodge of Elks, came to me and said:

"Kel, there is to be a benefit tendered Dan Hurley at the Boston Theatre tonight. He is a fine fellow, and we want to give him a good house. Won't you have the Philadelphia and Boston clubs attend? After the benefit, we want you to come over to the Elks Club for a while. There is to be a little reception there."

I promised to do both, yet I never had an idea as to what was in store for me. After the benefit, accompanied by several friends, I went to the club. What a charming gathering it was. I was introduced to many gentlemen, and even then I hadn't the least idea as to what was the entertainment for the night. Finally, we went up stairs, and what a splendid banquet was prepared. I began to think, about the time I sat on the right of Mayor O'Brien, that something or other was up. Then, when the mayor had finished his speech, I knew all about it. In behalf of the Boston Lodge of Elks and other friends, he presented me with a handsome gold watch, chain, charm, and pencil. For the first time in my life I was unable to make a speech. I had faced angry mobs on the base ball field, and had made funny speeches to them, but, like the Waterbury clock man in "She," my tongue was paralyzed, for the first time in my life. I said something or other, I don't know what. It was the first present I had ever received. I had been a member of the Chicago club for several years, and was glad to draw just my salary. But I came to Boston, and the first day of my arrival was given a testimonial fit for a king.

Well, there is only one city in the country where they do that sort of thing, and that's in Boston.

In Chicago, the opening game of '87 was to be a very pleasant occasion. It led me to believe that pomp and pageantry are not always reserved for statesmen or warriors. The Boston club arrived from Indianapolis at six o'clock in the morning. A few hours after, an immense crowd of people gathered at the Leland House, where the nine were stopping. A reception was given me a few hours before we started for the ball field. A quartette sang some complimentary verses to my skill as a player, then the crowd wanted me to make a speech. But this I was unable to do, owing to the fact Eugene Field said, that I had a lame leg. At noon, the Chicago club arrived at the hotel, and escorted us to the ball grounds, a band and a big crowd followed in the rear. That afternoon I received an immense floral tribute, composed of hundreds of roses and carnations, and bearing this inscription in red immortelles:

"KEL"

Several other floral pieces I received, and later, a jockey's cap made of red, white, and blue silk, came from friends. There was lots of cheering from twelve thousand people who were present, all of which convinced me that I had a good many warm, staunch friends in Chicago. The newspapers contained columns of matter in regard to the reception. But it was all of such a complimentary nature, that I cannot reproduce it here. One of the best things written at the time, was from versatile Eugene Field, of the Chicago *News*. He printed the following story:

Mr. Michael J. Kelly, the eminent base ball virtuoso of Boston, has been the recipient of many flattering attentions at the hands of Chicago literati since his arrival in this city last Friday. He accepts all courtesies with the same modesty of demeanor which characterized Col. James Russell Lowell's career in Chicago last February. In fact, all Boston men seem to be alike, when it comes to the particular of modesty.

"I like Mr. Kelly better than I do Lowell," says Col. Samuel J. Bosbyshell, the Prairie Avenue millionaire. "When Lowell was here, I had him out to the house to a $3,500 dinner, and, do what I could, I couldn't get him waked up. He didn't seem to want to talk about anything but literature. Now, when I'm out in society, I make it a point never to talk shop, and

Lowell's peculiarity mortified me. If it hadn't been for Frank Lincoln, with his imitations and funny stories, the dinner would have been a stupid affair. But Kelly is another kind of man; he is more versatile than Lowell; I don't believe he mentioned books once during the four hours we sat at dinner last Saturday evening. Nor did he confine his conversation to base ball topics. He is deeply versed in turf lore, and he talked most entertainingly of the prominent race horses he was acquainted with, and of the leading jockeys he has met."

Mr. Kelly himself was in fine spirits yesterday. He spent most of the morning writing letters to eastern correspondents. One of these letters was to the venerable A. Bronson Alcott, the recondite and erudite philosopher.

"Just before our second game in Indianapolis last week," said Mr. Kelly, "I received a long letter from Alcott, urging me to attend the school of summer philosophy at Concord, next August, and to read a paper on that occasion. Of course my professional duties will not admit of my accepting the invitation, but as the only paper I ever read is the *Daily News*, almost anybody can take my place."

Mr. Kelly went on to say that he was charmed with life in Boston; he had been most cordially welcomed by the leading society circles, and had in five months become so thoroughly Bostonian that he could hardly realize that he had ever lived in the wild and wooly West.

"You have no idea," said he, "how different everything is there. Chicago people boast of their lake, of their Board of Trade Building, of their parks, and of their refinement; but in each of these particulars, Boston can knock the socks clean off'n Chicago. We have a natural lake located just off Boston, that is, well, say ten times bigger than Lake Michigan, and it doesn't have to be dredged every three days to give the schooners enough water to sail in. Then there is Bunker Hill Monument; why, it is three times higher than your Board of Trade steeple, and Boston Common was old enough to vote long before the buffaloes had got through making a stamping-ground of your Lincoln Park. As far as social advantages are concerned, Boston heads the league. It is the oldest city in America, having been founded in less than a fortnight after Christopher Columbus anchored the Maypole off Plymouth Rock. Everybody speaks all sorts of languages, and attends lectures, and reads poetry, and wears spectacles. I hadn't been in the town more than two days before I got a craving for literature, and I couldn't get any peace until I had subscribed for the 'Waverly Magazine.'"

"I lived so high," continued Mr. Kelly, "that I got the gout; at least I thought it was the gout. One of my toes swelled up as big as a nut-cake, and was as sore as a bone falon. I went to see Dock Holmes about it; maybe you've heard of Holmes; he had written books, and enjoyed a large practice at public dinners in Boston for a good many years. Well, he examined my feet, and they seemed to interest him."

"'Mr. Kelly,' said he, at last, 'you have two of the most poetic feet I ever scanned. They are of a kind rarely to be met with nowadays. The left one is a pyrrhic, and the right one (with the bay-window on it) is a spondee.'

"'Is it — are they serious?' I asked, for I hadn't been in Boston long enough to know what this sort of thing meant.

"'A pyrrhic foot,' says he, 'is too short; your left foot is clearly pyrrhic. A spondee is too long, and that's what your right foot is.'

"'Jiminy Chris'mas!' says I, 'what shall I do about it?'

"He gave me a bottle of pain-killer, and told me to rub it twice a day on the spondee. It has done me a power of good."

"Did you meet Mr. Lowell in Boston?"

"Yes, but he's in Europe now, you know," said Mr. Kelly. "I called on him when he got back from Chicago. He told me that one of the Chicago clubs knocked him clean out of the box. He was badly rattled, but I braced him up a good deal, and me and him got to be great friends."

Mr. Kelly said that it made his heart ache, to see so many bright men groveling around in dirty, commercial Chicago, when they would be appreciated, and could do so well, in Boston.

"I met Joe Medill the other day," said he, "and I told him that he ought to be ashamed of himself, to vegetate here on the prairies, when a big reputation and big money were waiting him down East. He asked me what I meant, and I told him that if he'd let me work it for him I'd get a Boston editor to pay $10,000 for his release, and guarantee him $5,000 a year. Now, I suppose he thought I couldn't do it; at any rate, he smiled sort of sick like, and said that inasmuch as he had got started in here, he guessed he'd better pass the evening of his life in Chicago."

Perhaps the most exciting games of ball played in late years were the games between the Detroits and Chicagos, in the season of '86. McCormick and I had won seventeen straight, successive victories, and the Detroit club had won eighteen straight on the home grounds. We went to Detroit, accompanied by hundreds of Chicago lovers of the game. They all carried new brooms; and even the little boy mascot of the Chicago club marched on the field with us with a big broom perched over his right shoulder. How the men from Chicago did cheer! What a tremendous noise the "Hoosiers" did make! They cheered every player of the home club every time that they came to the bat. But McCormick was in great trim, and so were the members of the Chicago club. As a result, we won the first game. The men from Chicago were wild with enthusiasm. They coated the town of Detroit with paint of vermilion color. It was well they did, because on the next two games they didn't have a chance. The Detroit giants made a great race, and won both games.

The following three games between the two nines were played in Chicago. The club from Detroit came to Chicago with a tremendous backing. They had at least five hundred enthusiasts with them on a special train. On this train some of the most enthusiastic had a big tally-ho coach, painted red, and covered with flags and bunting. That was George Muchmore's idea. George is a Detroit boy, and a brother-in-law of President Stearns, of the Detroit club. He is a splendid fellow, and is known and is popular throughout the country. The idea was to have some of the best known men in Detroit jump into this coach and parade around Chicago, burning red fire, in the evening, providing of course, that Detroit won. But man proposes and God disposes. The Detroit men, both on and off the field, worked hard for victory. But Chicago was in great condition, and won three straight games. It badly demoralized the Detroit players, and the lovers of the game went back to the Wolverine city, sadder, but wiser men.

That tally-ho coach never left the train till it was taken off again at Detroit.

"What do you think of it, George?" I said to Muchmore; "do you think Detroit will win the championship this year?" "Well, Kel, I don't think we will this year," said Muchmore, sadly; "but I'll wager you a new hat that the pennant will be ours in '87."

George had sand.

Chapter XII

If you are an admirer of base ball, you will carefully read this chapter, and if there is any little moral in it, please remember it next summer, when you are excited about the success or failure of your favorite team. I want to say just a word about the umpires. It's an old subject, perhaps, and it may be a difficult matter to throw any new light upon it. But I will try it, hoping that a few timely words may be of some benefit to that much-abused class.

To begin with, umpires are human. They have a heart, and the blood which flows through their body isn't any different from that which flows through the body of the ordinary man. Very many men who attend ball games, sometimes forget this. They look upon umpires as creatures of their pleasure. They seem to think that they can abuse them, coddle them, make them think they're the smallest thing on earth, just as humor possesses them.

Did you ever sit near a man in a grand stand, who didn't feel certain that he could give an umpire points on the game? I never did. Some spectators see about two ball games, and then they feel certain that they can give an umpire advise in regard to points of the game, and how decisions should be made.

Now, it is necessary that an umpire should be pretty well posted on the game, before he is appointed. Sometimes, of course, a mistake is made, and a man is appointed who knows positively nothing about the game. But these appointments are few, and far between. An umpire must be somewhat of an athlete. He must be light on his feet, and be able to get around to the bases as quick as the batter. He must know all the rules of base ball, and give a prompt decision without looking at the book. His eye must be good, and he must be able to see all over the field at once. He must have good nerve, and if he wants to be a success, he won't allow any back talk from players.

Above all things, he must know more about base ball than the ordinary man. If he didn't, he would not be appointed.

The moment an umpire calls time, his actions begin to be closely watched. He is on the rack, so to speak. If his voice is a bit hoarse from howling "balls" and "strikes" for a couple of hours the day before, he is greeted with "louder!" from all over the grounds. If he leaves his position for a moment, to drink a glass of ice-water, or to wipe the beads of perspiration from his warmed-by-the-sun face, he is greeted with derisive howls, from somebody he displeased a moment ago.

Reader, think it over. See if you cannot remember several occasions similar to that one which I refer to.

He carefully watches every point in the game. Nothing escapes him, unless it's the "roasting" he received from the spectators around first and third bases. He does try to forget that.

He may make a wrong decision now and then.

Well, suppose he does? Does it improve matters any for a crowd to howl and shrick itself hoarse, hurling strong adjectives at one man?

It doesn't make him any fairer. Not a bit of it. In fact, it hurts his judgment very much, indeed. He may go to work to create good impression, and give the other side a decision, to atone for the bad one of a moment before. Then the crowd begins to shrick again, and perhaps the umpire gets rattled. His judgment becomes very bad. Then the crowd is after him, and life is a burden to him until the game is over. It's bad enough for the umpire to get a "roasting" from the players, but when the audience begins to get its work in, then it's very, very rough, indeed.

There are good players in every club, who make it a point to abuse the umpire, just to get the sympathy of the crowd. Perhaps a player might have reason for it, once out of ten, but as a rule, he hasn't.

The umpire is placed in a false position by the player, and gets abuse. The player gets the sympathy of the crowd, and applause.

This should be prevented, if possible. To be sure, there should be good umpires. But when good ones are in the market, they should be offered inducements enough to remain in the business. They should be given a good, big salary, and a fair show. An umpire like Gaffney or Doescher, should be worth at least $2,500, and even as high as $3,000. It's a pretty high figure, but it should be paid, just the same.

They get abuse enough in the course of a season, to make $2,500 a very slight salary, indeed. An umpire isn't there to give clubs the worst of it all the time. He is there to be as fair to one side as the other. He may make a rank decision once in a while, but don't get excited, if he does.

Keep quiet, and the result will be, that you will see better ball playing and better umpiring.

"Baby" Anson is a great kicker, but I will wager that there isn't an umpire in the country who doesn't like and respect him. Anson never kicks hard, or abuses an umpire. He wins him more by kindly argument.

An umpire's lot isn't a very happy one. So don't go to work next summer making a business of making one man's life miserable.

Give the umpire a square show for his life. Don't howl at him. Don't imagine that you know it all and he nothing. Don't think that he is robbing your club of a game. Don't get mad. Don't think that he was appointed simply to give decisions to suit you.

Don't do these things; and the result will be, that you will see better games of ball.

Chapter XIII

Who are the greatest pitchers in the league?

This question, I think, is determined entirely by locality.

For instance, New Yorkers will swear by Tim Keefe, and say that he is the greatest pitcher in the league. He is a great pitcher, and can fool the heaviest batters pretty often. Keefe has a way of covering the ball so that it is almost impossible for a batter to know just what sort of a ball is coming. Welch, of the same nine, is also a great pitcher. Mickey's friends say that he is the best, while Keefe's stick to him. I have seen Welch pitch some wonderful games, but on the whole, Keefe, I think, is the greater of the two.

In Boston we have some good pitchers. I don't know whether or not Radbourn will be a member of the nine next year. I hope that he will be. I have always said that he is one of the very greatest pitchers in the country. I see no reason to change this opinion. Radbourn pitched in pretty hard luck for a time last season. The rules were all against him. How could he expect to be great, under the circumstances? I know for a fact that he pitched several games in Boston when unfit to do so, by reason of illness. Radbourn is a curious fellow. People who do not know him, have an idea that he is surly, but he isn't. He is a cool, deliberate fellow, isn't lazy, and isn't surly. He is very peculiar, but once understood he is a good fellow, and a good friend. There is no doubt but that he is a great pitcher.

There are two great pitchers in the Pittsburg club, Galvin and McCormick. Both of these men have seen service, and lots of it. I was with McCormick, and caught his delivery for several years. He has few equals in this country. Ferguson, of the Philadelphias, is a very tricky pitcher, and a good pitcher, in the bargain. Buffinton, of the same club, is a young fellow who pitches a pretty stiff game of ball. He uses good curves, and his down shoots are particularly effective. The great trouble with Buffinton is that he sometimes gets mad, and loses his temper. Now Ferguson never does that. He might appear to, but he doesn't. Buffinton is a hard worker, a good, faithful player.

There are many who may not agree with me, but I have an opinion that Baldwin, who the newspaper boys have styled "Lady" Baldwin, is the star pitcher of the Detroit club. Put him in a winning game, and he does great work. Let the opposing nine bat him pretty freely for a few innings, and he goes to pieces. He loses heart. That is all he lacks to be a great pitcher. Getzein, of Detroit, is a strong, bull-headed pitcher. He doesn't lack heart, but he does sometimes lack head, but not very often. He pitched great ball last year, because he was in a great team. In an inferior team, perhaps he wouldn't be so great. However, he did good work, splendid work, and he should be given lots of credit for so doing.

Among the youngsters in the league, there are none so promising as young Madden, of the Boston club.

That lad was a mystery to me during the season of '87. I honestly expected to see him go to pieces half a dozen times in the course of some games, but he didn't. It used to send a cold shiver down my back when he faced Thompson, Brouthers, Connor, and many of the other big batters. But he was always game. He faced them like a little man. That boy has heart enough, and nerve enough, for a man twice his age. If William Stemmyer, of the Bostons of '87, had half of Madden's heart, he would be the greatest pitcher in the league.

John Clarkson is the star pitcher of the Chicago club, and by many people is looked upon as the star pitcher of the league. Clarkson is a quiet, modest gentleman, and does less talking about base ball, than any player in the country. He has all the essential qualifications necessary in the make-up of a great pitcher. He has a good long head, and knows how to use it. He has good judgment, and he displays it all at critical times. His command of the ball is simply wonderful. He has more curves and shoots than any pitcher in this country. There isn't a heavy batter in the league who likes to face Clarkson at a critical moment. He will keep them thinking, and the chances are ten to one that he will fool them on a deceptive ball. Van Haltren, of the Chicago club, is a good pitcher, and in time he is apt to be a great one. He is a bit wild at times, but will soon get over that.

Who is the best pitcher in the league?

Which is your favorite?

Well, he is the greatest!

In regard to the batsmen, it's a pretty difficult matter to say which is the best. You can give the names of those who have led the league during the various years. But it doesn't necessarily follow that they are the greatest in the league. There are some men who never led the league, or who never got anywhere near the top; yet they are great batters. They are great at critical moments. They can hit the ball when a run is needed. Those are the men that I regard as great.

Little Miller, of the Pittsburg club, can send the ball pretty far away when it's necessary. John Burdock, of Boston, is a good sacrifice hitter, therefore a good batter. Martin Sullivan, of the Chicagos, has improved as a batter, and he will go to the front before many seasons. Young Ryan, of the same team, has been doing good stick work. Dalrymple, George Gore, McCormick, Burns, and "Buck" Ewing are all bad men facing a pitcher.

Sam Wise, of the Boston club, is a player who is quite handy with the stick. Sam isn't a sure batter, but he does give the ball some terrible hard knocks. If Sam doesn't strike out, you may feel pretty certain that he's going to line out a three-bagger. Fred Pfeffer is a safe batter. Johnny Ward, of the New Yorks, is a very scientific batter. Ward can bunt the ball, or send it far into the outfield, whenever occasion requires. Billy Nash, of the Boston club, is coming to the front as a heavy batter. Nash meets the ball like a veteran, and when he hits it, one can make up his mind that it is going pretty well into the field.

Wood, of the "Phillies," is a good, strong batter, and so is Paul Hines. I like to see the latter come to the bat in an emergency. He always goes up to the plate as though he meant business. He generally does, too. Glasscock is a fine batter, especially if he is in a good nine. Jerry Denny hits the ball often, and hits it hard.

It will be interesting to many to know the records of the men who have led the leagues.

Roger Connor, the crack first baseman of the New York Base Ball Club, held the batting championship in 1885. Like all of the leading batters in the league, he is of immense stature, and is a favorite all over the country. He stands over six feet in height, and weighs over two hundred pounds. Roger hails from Waterbury, Conn., and first played with the Monitors, of that city, in 1876. He joined the New York club in 1883, and has been with that club ever since. His play at first base has always been up to the highest mark, and he has no superior as a heavy hitter. He is a good runner, and the appellation has been applied to him, that when he is running the ground trembles. He is a perfect gentleman, both on and off the ball field, and is a valuable member of the New York team. Connor stood second in the batting list of 1883, sixth in 1884, and first in 1885, his average being .361, .316, .371, in the order named.

James O'Rourke, the crack fielder and catcher of the New Yorks, who is going to be a great lawyer by-and-by, headed the list of league players in the batting records of 1884. He is a native of Bridgeport, Conn., and first played with the Osceolas, of that city, in 1871, as catcher. In the season of '72 he joined the Mansfields, of Middletown, Conn., and the following entered the ranks of professionals, by joining the Bostons, playing in right field, and as change catcher. During the six years he remained with the Bostons, he played every position in the out and in field, as well as doing valuable work behind the bat. In 1879 he joined the Providence team, and returned to Boston the following year, and finished the season there. He became manager of the Buffalo club in 1881, and remained there until 1885, when he joined the New York team as centre fielder. In 1886 he did excellent work behind the bat, when two of the catchers were temporarily laid up. O'Rourke is above medium height, and is ranked as one of the best all-around players in the profession.

Everybody knows Dan Brouthers, the genial, good-natured, whole-souled baseman of the Detroit team. Dan held the champion batting records of 1882 and 1883, playing first base with the Buffalo club, and to look at him, few would wonder that he is such a great batter. He stands six feet one and three-fourths inches in height, weighs two hundred pounds, and is as active as a cat. Brouthers first saw the light of day at Sylvan Lake, N. Y., in 1858, and in 1876 joined the Actives, of Wappinger Falls, N. Y., as pitcher. In 1878, he filled the box for the local club at Spattsville, N. Y. He entered the fold of the national league the following year, as first baseman and change pitcher for the Troys. The season of 1880 found him with the Baltimore team, but this club disbanded in June, and Dan went to the Hop Bitters team, but a month later was back with the Troys. In 1881 he signed with

Brooklyn, to play right field. He finished the season as left fielder. He joined the Buffalo club as first baseman, and remained there until his transfer to the Detroits, in 1885. In 1886, on the Boston grounds, Brouthers hit a ball over Sullivan's tower, which used to tower away above the fence erected by the Boston management, giving enthusiasts a chance to see the game for fifteen cents. That tower was pretty high up. The ball went over it, however, and away into Tremont Street in the bargain. I don't know anything about it, but I have an idea that that ball hasn't stopped rolling yet.

Few, if any, of the players in the base ball profession, are more widely known than Capt. A. C. Anson, of the Chicago team. His long connection with the White Stockings, his ability as a team captain, and his rarely erring judgment as to the qualities of a ball player, have made him an object of special prominence in base ball circles. He is a powerful fellow physically, standing six feet two inches tall, and weighs two hundred and eighteen pounds. Anson is without question, the best average batter of the league. According to the official records, he has stood first in the list of batters, three times; second, four times; fourth, twice; fifth, twice, and sixth, once; having never stood lower than sixth since his connection with the league. Anson is thirty-five years of age, and his first engagement was with the Forest City club, of Rockland, Ill., in 1871. The Athletics, of Philadelphia, secured his services in 1872, accompanying the club to Europe in 1874, where he made the highest individual score in the cricket match against the All Ireland Eleven. In 1876 he joined the Chicago club, and had remained with them since. He holds the batting championship for the season of 1887. Anson is admired by everybody for his management of a ball team.

Chapter XIV

There are so many different ways for a man to train, that it is almost utterly impossible for a man to tell which is best. Every athlete has his own idea. The base ball player has his, and he won't change. Neither will the oarsman, the pugilist, the pedestrian, or the other athletes. There are almost as many different ways to train, as there are athletes in this country. John L. Sullivan confines his training almost entirely to jogging along roadways, taking short runs, and punching the bag. In this way he generally manages to get himself in very good condition. On the other hand, Hanlan, the oarsman, does his best work in a boat. He rows morning and afternoon, and also takes other exercise. He was the most faithful training man in athletics a few years ago, but of late he has grown stout, and has been inclined to neglect certain things. This may account for his failure to retain championship honors. It is necessary that an athlete should take the very best of care of himself, even when he is not preparing for an athletic event.

There is a class of people who rarely exercise, and it's a fatal mistake. There isn't a man in the world strong enough to live a long life, and be healthy, without taking proper exercise. How many business men we know, who at fifty complain that they haven't any appetite. They complain in the morning, that they cannot eat; for lunch, a plate of soup, and several glasses of brandy is the best they can do; at night, for dinner, they have a little of this or that, but, as a rule, the soup and the liquors make up the best part of their meal. This should not be so. Every man should exercise in moderation. It is a necessity. Try it, and at the end of a year you will discover how much better you feel. I give a few hints on training, at the urgent solicitation of friends, and because of letters I have received from people I have never met. Do not try them all. Pick out the one you like best. Exercise, even if it's only a two-mile walk each day.

While no set rules can be laid down for training, some useful points can be given to beginners, which, if followed closely, will not fail to produce the desired result. Some years ago, a code of rules was laid down for training, and they were thought to be complete. Experience, however, has proved otherwise, and the several trainers were not long in finding it out. So the latter put their heads together, studied their men, and found out just how much they could stand. The solution of the problem was solved, and the men began to improve, and the standard of athletes to rise. So the reader will see that a man may be given all of the points on training, yet he will never obtain the desired result, until he makes a careful study of his own system, and finds just how much work will bring him to the pink of condition.

A great many people labor under the idea that training is a fearfully arduous and trying ordeal, and they wonder why men should undertake such a task for the honor to be derived from victory. Such, however, is not the case. To any athlete who likes his work, training is an easy task. The trouble is that too many athletes have, during the intervals between seasons, neglected to take proper care of themselves, and go round dissipating and carousing to such an extent that training to them means little more than hurrying their system in proper condition by ridding it of the alcohol with which they have become saturated. Good, honest training is not a hard task, by any means, but, on the contrary, is a pleasure, as a man never feels so well as when he is in perfect condition.

There is one fundamental rule which must be followed in all training, and that is, to thoroughly cleanse the stomach by a strong purgative. No matter how strong and healthy a man may be, this is the first part which must be accomplished, before anything further can be done. After this is done, the athlete is ready to begin good work.

I will take up the training of the pugilist first. He rises at an early hour, and takes a smart walk of a mile or so before breakfast. This gives him a hearty appetite, and he can eat his breakfast with a relish. A chop or a slice of beef cooked rare is generally given, but oatmeal mush is a nutritious and strengthening article. Breakfast over, a good long walk and jog follows. A suit of heavy clothing is put on, with heavy boots. If the man is fat, and has a lot of superfluous flesh, the heaviest kind of clothing should be put on, while a strip of flannel tied tightly across the stomach will serve to reduce that member. The walk should not be too long, as a wearying journey is likely to bring a reaction, in the shape of loss of vital energy, and staleness, which, above all things, must be avoided. A short distance at a good lively trot is by far the best plan, as fast work draws out the perspiration, and hardens the muscles of the legs. On returning, the damp clothes should be taken off as soon as possible, and the skin rubbed down first with rough towels, so as to thoroughly dry the surface, then with bare hands, and finally with rum, alcohol or some other ingredient.

When the rubbing down process has been completed, and it should be done thoroughly, since more superfluous flesh can be rubbed off than run off, the athlete is pretty tired. He is then wrapped in warm blankets, and allowed to sleep until dinner-time. For dinner, good, substantial food should be taken, and one should not stint himself. The old English idea of starving an athlete has long since exploded. If one requires a stimulant, a bottle of Bass' ale is the proper thing. After dinner, comes the gymnasium work. The athlete strips, and a good long time is spent in pounding the football, which is suspended from the ceiling. This not only serves in strengthening the muscles of the arms and stomach, but it loosens the muscles of the shoulders, thus giving free action, and enabling the fighter to strike a good, clean blow, free from muscle binding. This over, the rubbing down process is again gone through with, and the pugilist dons his clothes, and starts for a stroll before supper. After this meal, which should be a frugal one, work is over for the day, and the athlete soon seeks his couch. This work is continued daily until a short while before the fight takes place, and then gradually lessened. The minor details, such as hardening, etc., are of but small importance, and I will not relate them here.

The rules for training for a contest at wrestling cannot better be given than by describing the training process of William Muldoon, who is probably the king of Graeco-Roman wrestlers of the present day. Muldoon says:

"I have my own ideas on the subject of training, and while they may differ from others, I have found them effective, when put to practical use. When training for a contest, I rise very early, and take a short walk before breakfast. After that meal is over, I put on heavy clothing and start out for a breather. I run about three miles, say a mile and a half out and back, and go at a good fast pace. I am not an advocate of long and tedious travels. I see by the cablegrams from Europe, that Sullivan is doing his twenty miles a day. I don't believe in that. If Sullivan is really doing that amount of work, he will wear away some of that wonderful strength of his, and go into the ring with Mitchell a stale man. When I return after my run, I am thoroughly rubbed down with rough towels. After this, I dress and lounge around until dinner-time. After the noonday meal I take a short stroll, and then returning, strip, and prepare for practice. I always make it a point to have some one near me who is a pretty clever wrestler, and for quite a time in the afternoon I wrestle with him. This serves a double purpose. It not only tends to harden my muscles, and also reduce flesh, but it also gives me the practice I need, and is practical training which I have always been in favor of. This completes my day's work, and, after a light supper, I retire early."

Now, to the rules for a sprinter. As there are a goodly number of sprinters who work every day, and have to train during their leisure hours, so as not to interfere with their regular work, a course is mapped out below by which they may get into shape. After the cleansing of the stomach, an athlete should rest for a few days, so as not to weaken himself. After that, the regular work begins. He should make it a point to rise early, and, putting on a rough suit, take a short walk before breakfast. On his return, he should thoroughly rub down and put on warm, dry clothing. If possible, he should take a run in the morning. In the beginning, he should wear very heavy clothing, and it is also advisable to wear very heavy shoes, as they have a tendency to harden the legs, and at the same time to protect the feet form soreness. The sprinter should not run a long distance in the beginning, as fast work at that time will result in strained muscles and consequent soreness.

Too many beginners make this mistake. The first day they feel strong, and can do wonders. The novice does a vast amount of work, and when he leaves the ground feels "chipper." The next morning, however, when he rises, he finds himself so sore that he can hardly stand. He becomes disgusted, and his athletic career is at an end. By slow work at first, all soreness is avoided. The muscles are hardened gradually, and are ready for hard work when the time comes. After his work is once completed, the runner should leave the track at once, and rid himself of his wet clothing. Too many make this fatal mistake of standing around after work, the result being colds, and consequent soreness. After being thoroughly rubbed down with alcohol, or some other ingredient, one should dress rapidly, and take a short walk, so as to keep the muscles from stiffening. In the afternoon the same process should be undergone. After a few weeks of this kind of work one is fit for fast work, and the heavy clothing and shoes may be discarded for a light athletic suit, and spiked shoes. If a runner is practicing for one hundred yards, he should first move a short distance easily, so as to loosen the muscles, and then run his distance at a good, strong gait.

In starting, a man should always first take an easy position, with the left foot well forward of the right, so as to find just what "reach" he has. Then the position of each foot should be marked, and holes scraped in the track in these places. The holes give one a purchase to spring from, and also permit of a firmer footing, while waiting for the pistol shot.

The usual form of starting now in vogue is as follows: The starter first tells the men to "get on their marks," when they stand at ease in their places; the second command is to "get set," when the athlete lowers his body, with most of the weight resting on the forward foot, although the back foot should be firm, so as to be capable of allowing a good spring. Then follows the pistol shot, and the race is on. In springing from the mark, the back foot should come forward, and take the first step. The eastern amateurs are now affecting what is called the "dab," that is, a short step with the forward foot when the pistol cracks. This, however, has not been adopted by the best men.

In practice, the runner should go through the regular form, obtaining some one's services to give the word. After a siege at starting, the runner covering about thirty yards at each attempt, a spin of one hundred and twenty-five or one hundred and thirty-five yards completes his work. The same work should be taken in the afternoon. If one finds himself getting stale, a few days' rest will restore his form.

The question of diet is one that bothers many. Training should make but little change in a man's diet. Pastry and greasy food should always be avoided. With regard to stimulants, it can be said that a man unaccustomed to drinking needs no stimulants. A little sherry and egg before breakfast, or a bottle of ale, will do no harm. A few days before the race, a let-up should be taken in training, so that strength can be gathered for the contest. These few points, if closely followed, will prove of wonderful assistance to young amateurs. There is nothing theoretical about them, but the practical application of them has proven, beyond a doubt, their effectiveness.

Chapter XV

I am a firm believer in the boys of America. If I could afford it, I would allow all the small boys, of high or low degree, to witness the ball games free of charge. The small boys are a tower of strength to the game of base ball. Perhaps the revenues of the club are not made rich by their presence at the league games. Perhaps they do go "junky" (that is, pick up old waste paper and junk) during the morning hours, for the purpose of getting pennies enough to go on a shed to see a ball game; perhaps they do make life a burden to grownup men, asking for pennies to take them in; perhaps they do pick out the favorite knot-holes in the fence, and fight for their possession against bigger and stronger boys.

They do all these things. Yet, on the other hand, look at the great good they do. They know the names of almost every player in the league. The chances are, that they know more about my season's record than I do myself. The same may be said of the other players. They read every scrap of matter printed in the newspapers about the players. They go home at night, and talk base ball to their fathers, mothers, sisters, cousins, and aunts. They make veritable gods of their favorite players at home. The result is, that the father has a strong curiosity to see these players. He may go alone, or he may take his wife or family, or even the small boy with him. If he is lucky, he will take the small boy with him.

Why?

Because the small boy will learn him how to score a game, and assist him in numerous other ways. He will tell him who the star players are. He will tell him who the best batter is, who can pitch best in the team, who can scoop in the high flies best, who can cover the bases in the quickest time, and one hundred and one other things which the parent never heard of, and which he would never hear of were it not for the bright, wide-awake, little fellow at his side. The parent begins to think more of his boy. He feels proud of the knowledge he possesses. He sighs to himself, observes, perhaps, that this is a progressive age, and thinks that at his age he never thought of base ball. He forgets that there wasn't a great base ball fever when he was a boy.

Then the small boy does another great service when he organizes a club. How many times have you stopped and watched him play his game on the village green, or the village common? How earnestly he enters into the spirit of his work. By-and-by you begin to grow enthusiastic. If there is a fence there you sit on the fence, and the chances are you will remain there until the game closes. Perhaps the boys are playing for a prize. May be it's for a cheap, twenty-five-cent bat. In a little while one side begins to go ahead of the other. Then, perhaps, you will see a follower of the club which is being defeated, attempt to make his escape from the field with the bat stuck down in the leg of his trousers. May be he is allowed to escape with his ill-gotten prize. Perhaps he is seen by one of the followers of the others side. If he is, you are going to see a good-sized scrimmage, and don't you forget it. You begin to grow very excited. First one club has the best of it, then the other. When the fight is all over, you leave your lofty perch, and go down to where the boys are, to separate them. But you make pretty sure that the fight is all over before you interfere. You might give them a short lecture, and in the midst of it some bright little fellow will say:

"What are yer given us? Say, we're playing for der championship, we are! What's that?"

You disappear, and feel that you're the smallest possible part of this great, big world. Well, the inevitable result is, that you begin to grow interested in base ball. The chances are, that you will go to the next professional game. You may go once, twice, thrice, and after that you are a regular attendant. You cannot help it.

Now a word to parents. If your boys become interested in outdoor sports, do not crush them. Do not tell them that they must stop. If they love boxing, do not burn up their boxing gloves. If they love foot-ball playing, do not put them to bed without supper, because they have a few bruises on their person. Try and remember that they are as proud of those bruises as you are of a new dress or a new suit of clothes. If they go boating, and fall into the water, do not spank them for wetting their old clothes. Try and think that it washed the clothes, and gave the boys a bath. Thank God that they were manly enough and strong enough to know how to swim. If they want to play base ball, encourage them in every possible manner. If you can afford it, buy them balls, and bats, and gloves, and masks, even uniforms, if you can. Put a base ball uniform on a boy, and you can starve him for a week afterwards. But while you are starving him, allow him to keep the clothes in the room with him. The moment he puts that uniform on, he's the proudest bit of humanity in all this world. Go and see him play ball, if you can, and tell him what a great player he's going to be. Encourage him in the sport. The profession of a ball player is just as honorable as law or the ministry, or anything else, if the player is honest.

Show me a boy that doesn't participate in base ball, or some other field sport, and I will show you a weak, sickly, hot-house plant, who will feel sorry, as he grows older, that he was ever born.

God bless the boys of America. I love them all. Why? Simply because I was a boy myself once. I'm a little older now, perhaps, and I might be looked upon as an old boy, but I'll remain a boy as long as I live. My boyhood days were a hard struggle for existence, but they were, nevertheless, the happiest and best days of my life.

Now, to my boy friends, and I hope I have many, I will give a few simple rules about the game: First, if you wish to become a good ball player, you must study hard, and go to school regularly. You must learn your lessons well, and obey your teachers. When school is over, go out and begin a ball game. Do not play with a soft ball. It is just as well to have a good hard one. It won't hurt you any more than the soft ball. When you see it coming to you hard, do not go out of the way, but rather go towards it. The harder it comes into you hands the least will be the damage. If you make an error, do not feel badly about it. Just make up your mind that you are going to do better the next time. Practice running, and especially how to make a good, quick start. Never close your eyes when you see a ball coming. Just keep them open, and say to yourself, "Well, here's a friend of mine coming; I'll stop him before he can do any harm." When you go to bat, make up your mind that you are going there to hit the ball. Wait until you get a good ball, one that suits you pretty well, and then hit it. Do not swing the bat around, as though you are going to break the ball. If you do that, you will never hit it. Just judge the ball as accurately as you can, and swing the bat gently. If the ball is coming quick, it won't require a great amount of strength to send it far out into the field. Then run for you life, and don't be afraid to slide, if a slide is necessary. The bones in your body are more limber than they will be half a dozen years hence. You can stand knocks as a boy, without the slightest harm to yourself, that would almost kill you as a man. Never run into another player, with the intention of hurting him. Never get angry, and never fight. Be manly, and only resort to fighting when you must do it to protect yourself. It isn't manly to fight. Boys, I'm a pretty old boy, and I only fought once in my life. That one was absolutely forced on me. Make up your mind that it's much better to run than fight. But if you run hard, and the other fellow is a better runner than you are, stop. Stop suddenly. Don't lose any wind. Just turn around and give him a good, sound thrashing. When it's all over, say that you are willing to shake hands with him. Then go home and tell your mother and father all about it.

Boys, just one more word. If you want to be successful in life, remember this:

Never do anything that you wouldn't have your mother know.

Chapter XVI

The idea of a second trip to San Francisco was suggested to me at near the close of the season of 1887. I was at Boston when New York parties wrote me, asking if I cared to go to California professionally, during the winter season. The work in Boston had tired me out pretty well, and I wasn't particularly anxious to go. I remembered the pleasure of a winter at Hyde Park, and felt that I would much rather be there. But I decided, just at the close of the season, that I couldn't very well refuse the offer, in view of the fact that it was very, very tempting. Contrary to the general understanding, I am not a millionaire. There are a great many people who think I am, but such is not the case. I shall never retire from the diamond for the purpose of living on the fortune which I have saved. If I did, I am afraid that I wouldn't have very long to live.

There are two classes of people whose wealth is always exaggerated by the great public. They are ball players and actors. I have been a ball player for several years; my debut as an actor, which was of recent occurrence, enables me to write knowingly on both subjects. There are a few rich ball players, and a few rich actors. But they are few and far between. They find so many different ways of spending money, that it is very hard for them to save very much. The difference between them is this: The actors are the popular favorites in the winter season, but in the summer time the popular fancy changes, and the actors take back seats. Both live in a constant whirl of excitement. Here today and somewhere else tomorrow. Striving to win the applause of the people. The cheers and huzzas from auditorium and grand stand are as bread and butter to a man dying of hunger.

Actors, like ball players, may tell you that they do not care for applause.

Accept this statement with the customary grain of salt. They want applause, and if they do not receive it they are failures.

Ball players are a big-hearted, good-natured set, and, as a rule, are friendly toward each other. If Tom is in rough luck, and needs money to bridge him over his troubles, Jack and Bill will come forward and give him half, perhaps more than half, of all the money they possess. It's a noble trait, and I am proud to be able to speak of it. They are public property, so to speak, and, like all public men, they have to spend almost as much money as they earn.

Perhaps you will shrug your shoulder, and say that they are spendthrifts. Not at all. Send a poor man to Congress, and let him have but his $5,000 a year salary. He is going there with the intention of living economically. Well, he thinks all the time that he is economizing. At the end of the year go to him and say, "How much money have you saved from your magnificent salary?" He will look over his accounts; he will tell you he didn't owe a dollar when he came to Washington. The chances are that he is from $500 to $1,000 in debt at the end of his first term. He wasn't extravagant, he feels sure of that. He has had but two suits of clothes during the year. Where did it go to?

A public man has one hundred and one different ways of getting rid of money. In the first place, there are the friends of his youth. They see him pretty often, and they are always needy. He cannot refuse. There is the private subscription paper. He doesn't like to be called mean, therefore he cannot refuse. He must purchase tickets for balls, give so much money to the agents for different charitable institutions, and last, but not least, he must look after his own family. These things, and a good many others of a similar nature, which I might refer to, keeps the ball player, as well as the politician and actor, from ever being rich.

So, when the last offer came for me to go to 'Frisco, it was so good that it was impossible for me to refuse. The club met at Jersey City. It consisted of Johnny Ward, Buck Ewing, Roger Conner, Danny Richardson, Tiernan, Brown, Jerry Denny, and myself. Mr. Ward was accompanied by his wife, well known to the American public as Helen Dauvray, and I by my wife. Mrs. Ward is a lady of lovely presence, and is a general favorite with many of the very best people in this country. She is talented and bright. Mr. and Mrs. Ward deserve every happiness. If they get all they deserve, they will, indeed, be the happiest couple in this wide world.

We left Jersey City on the night of Oct. 25. The following night we arrived in Cincinnati, where we attended the brotherhood meeting, which took place there the next day. Mr. Ward is an enthusiastic supporter of this organization. It was mainly through his advise and encouragement that the brotherhood became organized, and to him is due the credit of its being a strong factor in the national game. The base ball players were never so well treated as they are at the present time. The brotherhood has a great deal to do with this.

When the brotherhood meeting concluded, we journeyed on to New Orleans. Here we played several games of ball. We were very successful, and made considerable money. I always had a strong regard for New Orleans and its people. Some very pleasant hours were spent there, and some of the best friends I have live in that city.

We had a lovely (?) ride to New Orleans. Those of you who have travelled over the Queen & Crescent Railroad know what this means. Those of you who have not should be congratulated. We only passed through twenty-five tunnels, on a one hundred and ten mile journey. Just imagine us rolling in to the station six hours late. The train only met and killed fourteen cows on the journey. That journey I shall never forget. The cow-catcher did its duty nobly for a while, but finally the cows got the better of it. It was obliged to succumb. Finally the train did begin to put on speed, and before reaching New Orleans we were running at the rate of fifty miles per hour. It was enough to make a fellow's hair stand on end. How glad we all were when we landed in New Orleans. The first man that I met was Dan Owens. The ball players all know Dan. They all like him, too. He's such a splendid fellow that they couldn't dislike him, even if they wanted to. Another gentleman who was very kind to me, was George Prevazano. He is a base ball enthusiast, and all the ball players know him.

After being in New Orleans for several days, several of us accepted an invitation to go down to Mississippi to an old plantation, and shoot quail. Buck Ewing told me confidentially that he was a crack shot. I firmly believed him, because he never told me an untruth during all the time that we have been friends. I cannot rely quite so strongly on what Buck tells me hereafter. I confessed to him that I couldn't shoot very well, and I felt confident that all would be well, for he promised to show me how. We had guns, and plenty of ammunition.

We shot at quail and other birds, just seventy-four times. Out of that number, just three quail were brought to the ground.

Can you blame me, when I say that on that day I doubted Buck Ewing's veracity? Hereafter, he will tell others about his being a good shot, but never me. I remained on the plantation for four days. The other boys went on to Houston, Texas. They were there about three or four days before I arrived. During this time they had spent all their leisure moments in learning to ride broncho horses. They had succeeded pretty well by the time I arrived. They were all named after favorite jockeys. Imagine Roger Connor being named after little McLaughlin. Tiernan called himself Snapper Garrison, and Buck Ewing, who was English, you know, was Billy Hayward. Richardson said that he was patriotic to the backbone. He called himself after the jockey Murphy. Danny thought that Murphy was an Irishman. He didn't feel so good about the name a few days later, when the boys told him that Murphy was a colored boy. Dan didn't care so much about the color question, but it did bother him when the boys asked him if he was personally acquainted with "every jockey on this side of the water," a remark credited to Danny a few days before.

They had a fiery mustang all picked out for me when I arrived. I never rode on a mustang's back in my life, and didn't know what it meant. I had one experience, and that was about enough. I got a pair of stirrups somewhere. I put them on, because I was solemnly informed "it was the proper caper." Buck Ewing wanted to get me several guns to throw over my back. He said that if I did this, I would be the beau ideal of a cowboy. I reminded him of his remarkable shooting a few days before, and he desisted. I sat on that mustang's back quietly for a moment. Then, in gentle tones, I asked him to please go ahead. He wouldn't go, but, instead, preferred to kick his hind feet up into the air. I remonstrated with him, but it didn't do any good. The others all rode around me, and gave me advise. Roger Connor said the only way to win a horse was by kindness. I stood it just as long as I could; then I dug the stirrups into the mustang's side. He jumped, kicked, plunged, and reared, all at once. I had a pretty difficult time to hold my seat, but I finally succeeded. The stirrups became broken, and Ewing volunteered to arrange them for me. He tied them to my boots with shoestrings. I had just about all the mustang rides I cared for that day. When I was a boy, it was the dream of my life to ride a fiery mustang on the broad prairies. I have been astride the festive mustang. The dreams of youth were dispelled in a moment. I got all that I want, thank you.

Then we visited San Antonio, and saw the old, broken-down alamo where poor Davy Crockett was killed. It's an old castle, and our guide informed us that it was occupied by monks in the olden time. The great cathedral was also the object of a long visit. It's called the "Three Missions," I believe. It's a magnificent marble structure, and the people down there are justly proud of it. Los Angeles came next, and we crossed the Rio Grande. Another youthful dream dispelled. I thought it a grand, beautiful river. In many places I could jump across it in two jumps. We saw a good many Indians. They were lazy, peaceable, and dirty. They didn't wear any scalps at their belts, therefore they were not objects of special interest.

We arrived in San Francisco on Thanksgiving day. The opening game of the season attracted an immense gathering. You can imagine the crowd, when the proceeds were $5,200, at twenty-five cents each. We won several games, and received great treatment in 'Frisco. Harry Dixey, "Adonis," was playing there at the time. He was very kind to me. So was Chris Buckley, who is one of the political leaders of 'Frisco. Mr. Buckley hasn't the use of his eyes, yet they told me that he was a great political manipulator, and controlled considerable office patronage. He is a courteous gentleman, and to know him is to love him. He has been East several times, and he has friends all through the country. We remained in 'Frisco just five weeks. I came back overland with my wife. The trip was all right until I reached Albany. What a long ride it was from Albany to Hyde Park. Yet it's only a two hours' trip. That's always the way. The last hour of the journey seems like a week, especially when you are approaching home, sweet home.

Chapter XVII

How did I make my first appearance as an actor?

I have told you of the days when as a boy, I played in a Paterson cellar with Jim McCormick, but of the latter, and more important appearances, I have yet to write.

My first real stage appearance was at a benefit given Fred Vine, at Detroit. Frank Lane, the then well-known base ball umpire, who has since become a full-fledged actor, was in the cast.

The farce in which we appeared was called, "He would be an Actor: or the Ball Player's Revenge." I appeared as "Edmund Collier Anson," Frank Lane "Just a Moment," and C. W. Young as "Dr. Daniel O'Leary Landis." I didn't have very much to say, and I assure you that I said that quick. Captain Anson and the members of the Chicago club sat in a private box. The moment I came on they began to have their fun. The farce closed with Lane banging me over the back and shoulders with a clapboard. Captain Anson got excited. He leaned over the box and said, "Give it to him Frank, give it to him hard." I got it. The curtain went down and the farce was over.

This, however, was only my first appearance. It wasn't the most important, by any means. My first star engagement was at the Park Theatre, Boston, the week beginning March 26, 1888. This engagement was made in a very peculiar manner. Charlie Reed, who played "Old Sport," in "A Rag Baby," is a personal friend of mine. He wanted me to go on the stage, and play "Dusty Bob" with him, just for fun. I told him that at some future time I would surely accept his offer. The recent big blizzard in New York, you all remember. Well, I left Hyde Park and arrived in New York on Sunday morning. I was going to start for Boston the next day, to arrange several things in connection with my book. But I didn't start. The blizzard struck New

York Sunday night, and I remained at the Hoffman House for four days. Only once I left the hotel, and that occasion was to rescue my little dog "Nellie" from a snow-drift. In the Hoffman during the siege I met Charles W. Thomas, of Hoyt & Thomas, and little "Johnny" Ruddy, the "baby" manager. The latter is a charming fellow, and a dear personal friend of mine. Mr. Ruddy was very anxious for me to accept the part, and play it in Boston for one week. I felt like doing it, particularly as Mr. Reed was so anxious that I should. Finally I accepted, and promised to be on hand the next week for the rehearsals, providing, of course, the blizzard allowed me to get away from the Hoffman.

I had a very peculiar time attending the first rehearsal. Stage Manager Riddle called it for one o'clock in the afternoon, at the People's Theatre. I arrived there about fifteen minutes before one. I inquired at the box office for the stage manager, but was informed that he hadn't come to the theatre yet. So I went into the theatre, and took a seat in the orchestra. The curtain was down, and I was the only man in the theatre. I sat there for perhaps half an hour. It seemed like a year to me. I began to grow nervous, the awful silence of the place not being calculated to make a fellow feel pleasant.

Then I began to think of some of the players who had been on that stage. Why, what was that? Whisk! Up went the footlights, the little bell rang, and up went the curtain. Then the finest procession I ever saw came down from the centre of the stage. Why, there was the elder Booth. I remembered him from old cuts and photographs I had seen. Can that be John McCullough? Yes, that is the noblest Roman of them all. In what graceful folds did the toga cling to his manly form. His right hand was raised; his attitude denoted that he had something to say. That big, fine-looking man does look out of place between the two. Why, bless me, if it isn't "Charlie" Thorne! Why, I thought he was dead and gone! How handsome and upright he does look. This must be a joke; who is that, who just tripped on and caused the others to laugh heartily? He wears one eye-glass, and long, carefully combed whiskers. I've seen him somewhere; it's E. A. Sothern. Who wouldn't recognize our old friend "Dundreary."

"I'll match you," quoth a nervous, neatly-dressed little man, and I knew him at once. Poor John T. Raymond. That's strange. I'm sure that I read that he had passed over that great river. That is "Monte Cristo." How neatly he handles his sword. With what grace he removes his gloves. Charles Fechter's every motion is almost a poem. He is indeed great. There is another well-dressed man. How neatly and gracefully he carries himself. Why, its Captain Molineaux. No, it isn't; it's Harry Montague. What a splendid appearance he has. Now they all gather about a kindly looking old lady. "Ned" Sothern pats her lovingly on the cheek, and calls her "mother." She arranges a little curl on her forehead, and I recognize her at once. Who wouldn't? Why, its dear Mrs. J. R. Vincent. I wonder why it is she isn't at the Museum? She doesn't play at this theatre. It's all very strange. There is a stately looking woman for you. She is dressed in black, and a pair of gold-bowed glasses are suspended from about her neck. I've seen her somewhere. Why, of course I have! It's Charlotte Cushman. Then everybody is quiet for a moment, and the lovely Juliet appears. You have all seen her. It's Adelaide Neilson. She stops near the centre of the stage, and speaks in a low voice to the others. They reverently bow their heads, the thick drapery at the back of the stage parts, and a handsome gentleman in a costume of another century is revealed. William Shakespeare! Slowly he comes from his pedestal. Juliet falls to her knees, and in an impressive manner the great master places a laurel wreath upon her head.

There is a great clashing of music, the drum beats, the curtain begins to come down slowly; there is a mist; the actors disappear, and — I awake.

I'm shivering with the cold. I look at my watch. It's half past one. Guess the rehearsal is over. What a singular dream. How gloomy the theatre does look. With these thoughts chasing themselves through my brain, I leave the theatre in somewhat of a hurry. I feel gloomy for a moment, and would have thrown up all ideas of future rehearsing, were it not for the fact that I met Charlie Reed outside.

"Why, where were you, Kel?" he said. "We waited for you half an hour, and then dismissed the rehearsal."

"I guess not," I replied. "I've been in the theatre for half an hour. I've sat in the orchestra."

"That's a nice place to rehearse," said Reed, with elegant sarcasm. "The company was all waiting for you on the stage."

I went to the back door for all other rehearsals, and in future was as prompt as any member of the company.

Well, the opening night come around soon enough — too soon, for me.

All my friends were in the house, and it was packed from pit to dome. I was all made up when the first act began. I stood in the wings and watched the company. Every time Charlie Reed made the big audience laugh, it sent a cold shiver down my back. Then a young newspaper friend of mine walked on, and made a presentation speech to Mr. Reed. He escaped all right, and it gave me more nerve. "My turn now," I said, and before I knew it I was pushed on the stage.

"Where is the 'Old Sport?'" I roared, and then the noise began. The audience heard my first line, and then gave me the greatest reception of my life. The applause and cheers lasted nearly a minute. It seemed a year to me. Every time I bowed in acknowledgment I closed my eyes. I was afraid to look out into the auditorium. Finally I got a chance to speak the lines, and I did the best I could. I wasn't on the stage but five minutes, yet in that time I had lost five pounds. Every second that the applause continued, my knees would almost knock together. Stage fright? It may have been. It's an awful feeling. I would rather face ten thousand angry base ball enthusiasts on the diamond field, than go before a friendly audience in a theatre.

My first real appearance they told my afterwards was a success. I'm glad. Glad that it was a success; glad that I lived through it.

By this time most of you will have read of the fact, that John Clarkson, the Chicago pitcher, is to be a member of the Boston club next season. The Boston management worked hard to secure his release. Clarkson himself wanted to play in Boston, for several reasons. His wife and family lived in that city, and he was slightly homesick in Chicago.

At the conclusion of the last season, Clarkson informed Mr. Spaulding that he would not play in Chicago next season. Mr. Spaulding said that he certainly would, unless a sufficient amount of money was paid for his release. When Clarkson came to Boston, he told several of his friends that he did not care to play in Chicago. These friends so informed the Boston management, and it at once went to work to get his release, in an honest, honorable manner.

Right here, I would like to say just a word about the Boston management. In various parts of the country, ball players who never met Messrs. W. H. Conant, J. B. Billings, and A. H. Soden, have an idea that they are grasping men, who are looking for nothing but the mighty dollar, day in and day out. Such is not the case. There is not a more liberal management in base ball affairs, than that which directs the Boston Base Ball Club. I know just what I'm writing when I say this. They are modest gentlemen, and are not very well known to lovers of the game outside of Boston. Mr. Soden is the president of the club. He is rather short, inclined to be fleshy, and generally is cleanly shaven. He always wears a courteous smile, and is polite and attentive at all times. Mr. Billings is the treasurer of the club. He is rather nervous at times, but is goodhearted, and performs many charitable acts in a quiet, unostentatious manner. Mr. Conant is the best known of the directors. He is stout, wears a sandy moustache and chin whiskers; is invariably seen with a cigar in his mouth, and a cheery smile on his face. He loves to hear a good story, and he loves to tell one.

These three gentlemen control the Boston club. Unless I am mistaken, there are only two or three shares which they do not control. They are buying these shares up, and while they do not own them all yet, their power is as supreme over the other stockholders at that of the Emperor of Russia is over his subjects. They work always for the interests of the Boston club. It was for the interest of the club that they began to work for Clarkson's release. They felt confident that he was a great pitcher, and they wanted him in the Boston club. The first offer they made was $5,000, but Spaulding refused. The next offer was for $7,500; this was also refused. Mr. Spaulding knew his business. He knew that if Boston wanted Clarkson very badly, the Boston management would pay a comfortable sum for his release. Finally the Boston management sent its *ultimatum*. It said that it would give just $10,000 for the release of the Chicago pitcher. On April 3, Mr. Spaulding sent a despatch to the management, that the terms were accepted.

On the eve of my book going to press, the release of Mr. Clarkson was announced. I kept back the edition a few hours, for the purpose of speaking of the second grand deal. I met Mr. Conant, and in the course of conversation, he said to me, "Well, Kel, what do you think of the new pitcher?"

I replied that I considered him one of the greatest in the league.

"These twenty thousand batteries come high, Kel," said Mr. Conant, "but we must have the best, in Boston."

I wish that I had the space in this book to speak of the base ball writer of America. But I haven't, so I will have to bunch them all together. They have been more than kind to me in the past; I trust that I shall retain their favor in the future. O. P. Caylor, I know, is anxiously awaiting its publication. He is already sharpening his pencil, prior to putting on paper what he thinks of these few reminiscences. Perhaps he will like them so well, that he will ask me to continue to write reminiscences from Australia, or anywhere else that I may be stationed. My friend Bill Nye may attack my literary style, but I have always spoken well of him. I hope that he will remember that. Now, gentlemen, I thank you, one and all, for your many kindly acts. You have assisted me to the position I have won as a base ball player. I appreciate it all.

My little story is finished. I have tried to please you all, and hope I have been successful. I do not give you any records to pour over, nor do I take occasion to injure any gentleman in my profession. If the little stories help you to kill an hour of leisure time, and make you forget any little troubles, I feel that my task has been a success. The American public have been kind to me; more than kind, in fact, and I take advantage of the opportunity to thank you all from the bottom of my heart. Your applause and patronage of my humble efforts on the diamond have made this little book possible. To the press of America, I am also grateful. Were it not for this immense power, ball playing would never be popular, would never be the national sport. We owe newspaper men a great deal. I thank them, one and all. If they deal with me as kindly in the future as they have in the past, I shall be more than satisfied. What shall I say to my best friend, my greatest admirer, the small boy of America? To him I will simply say, "God bless you, my boy. 'Play Ball.'"

Appendix A: "Base Running" by M.J. Kelly, 1884

From *Wright and Ditson's Book on Batting, Pitching, Fielding and Base Running*

The department of base running is fully as important an essential of a game as the batting, and excellence in this department has gone far to remedy weakness at the bat. An examination of the work of batsmen will show that it is not always the player who makes the largest number of base hits that will make the most runs, nor will the fleetest runner be always the best base runner. A successful base runner ought to have a fast pair of legs as a foundation for success in this department, but many an example could be adduced of players who are not endowed by nature with this gift, but who are recognized as the best and worst daring of runners. They use their heads and study their men and chances. It takes experience to make a good base runner. It is not as a great many think, a mere matter of chance or luck. Pitchers and catchers work together so beautifully, perfectly and systematically, that the chances are wholly against a player's stealing second successfully. The system of signals has greatly enhanced the success of their work, for the catcher need not worry about the spot where to expect the ball. He is prepared to take the ball at once and forward it with the utmost dispatch to the second baseman, and in a perfect play, that player will be found waiting for the runner. When it is recollected how often one run is all that is needed to win a game, and how often this is thrown away wantonly, it will be seen how important it is to watch and seize every opportunity.

The runner should be perfectly cool and self-possessed; he should be sure to move only with a purpose; above all should he avoid anything calculated to please the crowd. This action is more often a failure than it is successful.

As soon as the player has hit the ball, he should make for the base with the utmost speed, and should not look either to the right or left. The worst thing that a player can do is to look about. If the ball is struck to the infield and is smartly picked up, it need not follow that it will be fielded as well, and to look about is detrimental to the chances of the runner. Never tarry; put for the base with all speed, as well on a third strike or six balls as after a hit. How many players have failed to run to first base after a missed third strike, and have been been put out, when by running immediately they would have been successful. And captains and managers do not enforce this injunction with sufficient strictness. The sixth ball may be a wild pitch or a passed ball, and a failure to make the most of this may result in obtaining but one base instead of two. Even on a fly ball, be sure to run as rapidly as possible, for a drop of a fly ball even in the infield will generally net two bases. But the runner should be careful not to force the runner ahead of him. Be careful not to make an effort to turn for second, after seven balls or on an infield hit, unless coached, or there is a plain chance to secure another base. On a safe hit or fly this can be done safely. On a safe hit a player ought to take all the ground toward second that he can, for on a poor return he can occasionally steal second. But this should not be done recklessly.

In conclusion, watch your coach as much as is compatible with the preceding instructions. Obey his commands with dispatch, and without hesitation, no matter what your feelings may be. He is there to guide the runner, and often the least hesitation in following his guidance has proved ruinous. When several players are trying to coach, strike for the nearest point of safety. He the player ought to use his own judgment.

M. J. KELLY

M. J. Kelly, of the Chicago Base Ball Club is acknowledged to have no superior as a base runner. Even his style of batting is conductive to success in this department, for scarcely has he dropped his bat, than he is off for the

M. J. KELLY.

bag. He never fails to make the most of his opportunities, and his quick and finely trained perceptive powers rarely lead him into error, and enable him to successfully accomplish daring plays. Last season he crossed the home base more times than any league player; the number of runs credited to him being 120 in 107 games. He is well built for success in this department, and is a very quick starter as well as runner. His presence on a base is a source of dread to any battery, and opposing fielders have good reason to give vent to a sigh of relief when Kelly is out of the way. Kelly can cover the bases under favorable circumstances in about 15 seconds.

He was born in Troy, N. Y., Dec. 31st, 1857, from there he moved to Washington, D. C. when quite young, and commenced his first ball playing with the Keystone, Jr. Club. In 1875–76 his parents took up their residence at Paterson, N. J.; being still quite young, here he joined and played with the Olympics of this city as right fielder and catcher. In 1877 he went with the Buckeyes of Columbus, Ohio, and played as catcher, and in 1878 and '79, played right field and catcher for the Cincinnatis. In the fall of '79 he went to San Francisco with the Cincinnati Club, and when he returned, joined the Chicagos, where he has been ever since, playing at various times, positions of catcher, short, third base and outfield. He is a willing and plucky player, always ready to fill any position placed in by his captain. Being quick and lively in his movements makes him a favorite with the spectators.

STEALING SECOND BASE

Position No. E.

After reaching first base, be sure that the base is not left while the ball is in the fielder's hand. One cannot be too careful about this. Take all the ground possible; the more that is taken, the more will the pitcher be bothered. The distance that can be taken will depend greatly upon the style of the pitcher's delivery — his quickness of throwing. It is here that there is a competition between the runner and pitcher for mastery. It is the wonderful quickness of Kelly of the Chicagos in taking action that makes him the king of base runners. He often throws the pitcher off his guard by his seeming lack of a desire to steal. Unless the ball is hit, never look back, but make for the base. If the ball is hit to right field, fast base running will ensure two

Position No. E.

bases. If it reaches the second baseman before the fielder can get to that base, he should stop and endeavor to return to the bag, to prevent a double play. In his anxiety to prevent the runner from reaching first, the fielder may throw wildly and both men will be safe. It is not the runner that dances all the time around first, that is the best runner. He gets caught far more often than the player who spends his time in watching his chances.

SLIDING TO THE BASE—HEAD FIRST

Position No. F

This is the most dangerous method employed in stealing second base, and but few runners make use of it. Yet these daring individuals have been more proportionately successful in reaching the bag, by reason of a knack and a clever dive. They are better enabled to slide under the fielder and reach the base. This mode is apt to injure the runner in his body, externally or internally, and scar his face and hands, and therefore should not be attempted.

SLIDING TO THE BASE—FEET FIRST

Position No. G

This is the common mode in vogue with base runners, and is the safest. The runner should be prepared to slide for the base, but at the same time should be careful to look out for the coacher's cry of "safe" or "slide." Practice will give him the proper distance to slide, which will bring him under the player on to the base. Sliding is generally a necessary feat, for by so doing, less of the person is exposed.

TOUCHING BASES ON THE RUN

Position No. H

Be careful never to overrun a base without touching it. Remember that umpires are very careful to detect any slip on the part of a runner, and that his attention will be called to any failure of a player to touch a bag, by the other side. In running, touch the base on its outer edge, describing as much of a curve as may be desirable to bring this about.

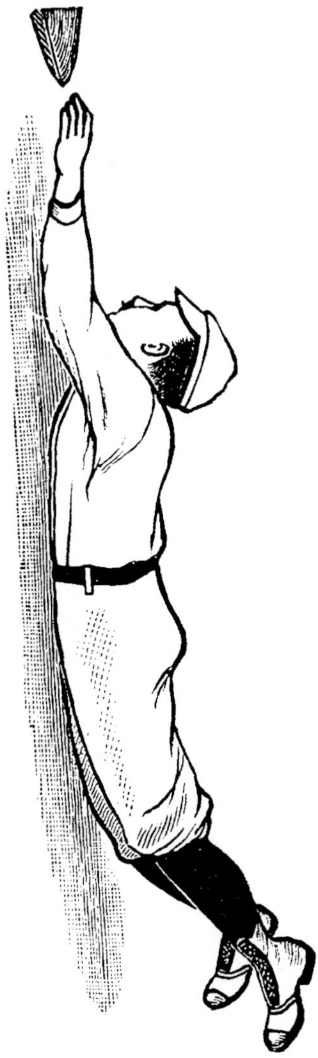

Position No. F.

Position No. G.

Position No. H.

Appendix B: "King Kelly, the Famous Catcher" by Billy Boxer

Chapter I. Mike Kelly As an Amateur

"Whew! But he can catch. Watch him."

"Who is he?"

"Don't you know Mike Kelly? Don't you know him?"

"No. Introduce me to him."

"I will."

The scene was a ball field in Paterson.

A number of young men and boys were engaged in a ball game, among whom was Mike Kelly, who was destined to be so famous on the base-ball field.

It was a bright summer afternoon.

It was a half-holiday with some of the operatives in the big factories, and hundreds of young men and boys watched Mike Kelly as he stood behind the bat.

It was an intermission in the game.

Charlie Hurd, a friend of Mike, addressed Ned Burns.

Ned was not acquainted with Mike. He had often seen him play ball, and wondered who he was.

"Permit me to introduce Mr. Burns, Mr. Kelly," said Charlie Hurd, as he walked to the catcher's box.

"I am very glad to meet you, Mr. Burns," said Mike. "I have heard a great deal about you."

"I am very glad to meet you, Mr. Kelly."

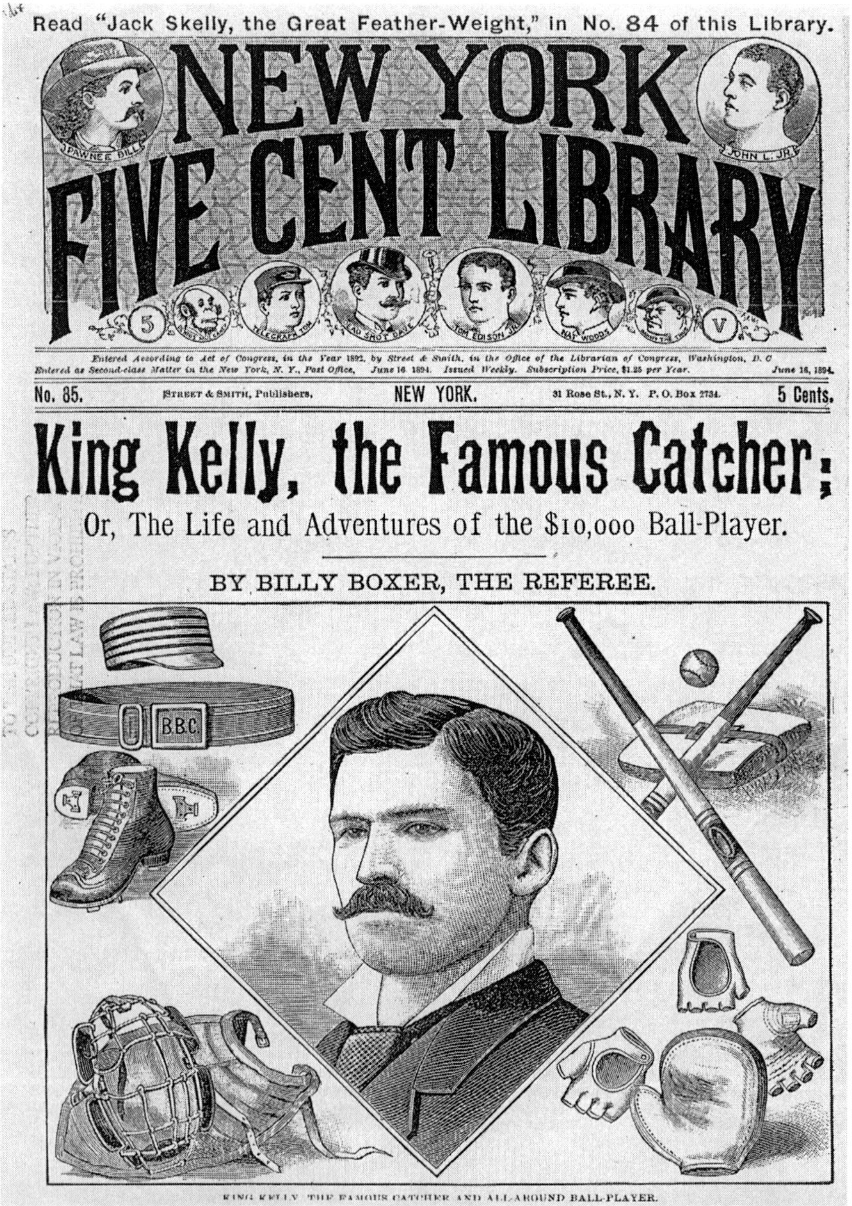

Read "Jack Skelly, the Great Feather-Weight," in No. 84 of this Library.

NEW YORK FIVE CENT LIBRARY

Entered According to Act of Congress, in the Year 1892, by Street & Smith, in the Office of the Librarian of Congress, Washington, D. C.
Entered as Second-class Matter in the New York, N. Y., Post Office, June 16 1894. Issued Weekly. Subscription Price, $1.25 per Year. June 16, 1894.

No. 85. Street & Smith, Publishers, NEW YORK. 31 Rose St., N. Y. P. O. Box 2734. 5 Cents.

King Kelly, the Famous Catcher;

Or, The Life and Adventures of the $10,000 Ball-Player.

BY BILLY BOXER, THE REFEREE.

KING KELLY, THE FAMOUS CATCHER AND ALL-AROUND BALL-PLAYER.

The two young men shook hands heartily.

Ned Burns had heard that Mike Kelly was a square, honest, upright ball player, and, as for Mike, he knew that Ned was perfectly on the level.

Mike had made quite a reputation as a catcher a long time before the opening of our story.

He had played with a number of clubs in and about Paterson.

His conduct had always been gentlemanly and kind to those with whom he associated, and he was wonderfully popular with every one he met.

"Hurray! Hurray! Hurray for Mike Kelly, the great ball player!"

"He's the greatest catcher in the world!"

These and other cries greeted Mike wherever he went.

"I am becoming quite popular," Mike said to Charlie Hurd, as they walked to and from the ball field to their homes.

"Yes, Mike, you're just in it," replied the other.

After the game that day, Charlie and Mike walked home together as usual.

When they neared the railroad depot, they ran across Eddie Carter.

Eddie was much younger than either Mike or Charlie, but both liked him because of his manly, courageous character.

"Hello, Eddie!" said Mike.

"Hello yourself, Mike Kelly!"

"You're as saucy as ever," said the other, as he laughed.

"I hope I'll never be saucy to you, Mike, because you have been so kind to me."

Eddie Carter's mother was a widow, who lived all alone on the outskirts of the town, and was very poor.

Mike had often helped Mrs. Carter, and in consequence Eddie thought there was no one like him.

As the two young men and Eddie walked along the street, Mike suddenly stopped and said, at the same time taking Eddie by the hand:

"How would you like to be my mascot, Eddie?"

Eddie's eyes were as big as saucers.

He did not expect such an honor.

To be Mike Kelly's mascot was the greatest thing in the world to him, and for a moment he could scarcely speak.

"Do you mean it, Mike?"

"Certainly, my lad. I always mean what I say."

"And I may be your mascot?"

"Yes."

It was decided that Eddie Carter should be Mike's mascot.

Every one in Paterson knew next day that Mike had taken an interest in Eddie, and they prophesied a great future for the boy.

"Mike is bound to succeed," said Charlie Hurd, in which opinion every one agreed.

There was a little working-girl named Katie Kane, employed in one of the big factories.

Between Mike and Katie a very friendly feeling existed.

Mike would meet Katie after her work was done, and walk with her to her home.

Mr. Kane, the girl's father, thought a great deal of him.

Up to this time the two had never acted toward each other, other than in a friendly way, but way down in the heart of each was a feeling that they might sooner or later become nearer and dearer to each other.

Chapter II. Mike Saves a Life

When Mike Kelly was not engaged at his business, he spent all his time in the ball field.

Day by day he was becoming more and more proficient.

Every one who saw him said he was one of the greatest catchers the country had ever seen.

"You had better look out, Mike, or you will find the League people will be after you," said Charlie Hurd, laughingly.

"I have no fear of that," said the other, good naturedly.

"Why not?"

"Why? Because the League managers would not take such a bum base-ball player as I am."

Yet Mike often thought that if he was chosen to become one of the League base-ball players he would be one of the luckiest men alive.

Often in the dead of night, he would wake with a start and see himself in the catcher's box with twenty thousand people shouting his name.

During these times he would lay awake and build castles in the air.

Often in his half-awake, half-asleep dreams, he would see base-ball magnates bidding for his services; but, when the morning light came, and he went about the duties of the day, he would say to himself:

"Pshaw! I will never be anything else than an amateur base-ball player."

As long as the light of the summer nights would permit, Mike Kelly played ball with his associates.

He had so great a following now that his fame was spreading to other towns and villages adjacent to Paterson, and hundreds of people would often come on a Saturday afternoon to see him catch.

Mike was happiest when he saw pretty Katie Kane in the grand stand when he was about to catch.

He imagined that the encouraging glances from her eyes made him surer of his hold on the ball, and when he threw to second, and some player on the opposite nine tried to steal second base, and the runner was put out, he smiled and waved his hand to the pretty girl.

One Saturday afternoon Mike was in greater form than ever.

The pitcher, a strong, clever man, did a large part of the work, but it was due to Mike's superior catching and throwing that the Paterson nine won.

When the Paterson boys were declared the victors, and the shouts of the people had died away, four of Mike's friends took him on their shoulders and carried him to the club-house.

"No one in it but Mike Kelly," shouted Eddie Carter.

"That's so. Mike is a great ball player," said Charlie Hurd.

Eddie and Charlie followed Mike Kelly to the dressing-room.

When Mike had taken off his brand-new gray uniform and natty blue cap, and had dressed himself in his street clothes he smiled.

"I am to see Katie Kane home," he said to himself.

When Mike, and Eddie, and Charlie had got outside the grounds Mike said:

"You will excuse me, boys, I know, won't you?"

Charlie and Eddie did not say anything.

They knew where Mike was going, and they watched the tall, broad-shouldered form disappear down the street.

"Well?" asked Eddie.

"Well?" asked Charlie, as he looked Eddie in the eyes.

As both spoke, they burst out laughing.

"Can you blame him?"

"Not I."

Both boys knew that Mike intended to meet Katie Kane and take her home.

Katie was walking slowly half a block ahead.

She had her eyes on the ground, and appeared in deep thought.

"Well, little one, how do you feel to-day?" asked Mike, as he came up behind her.

Katie gave a little scream.

She was so wrapped up in her thoughts, she did not hear Mike's footsteps.

"Oh, Mike!"

"Well, you haven't answered my question, little one."

This time the girl raised her eyes, and said:

"I have been very well, Mike. How have you been?"

"Oh! I am always well."

At this moment the two were walking through a very narrow street.

This street was so narrow that the authorities forbade trucks and carriages going but in one direction, the right.

If two trucks attempted to go through the street, one would have to take to the sidewalk.

Unconscious of any danger, the two walked slowly in the direction of Katie's home.

Katie was telling Mike how proud she was of him, and how glad she was to see him so popular.

"Father says you will become a great ball player some day."

Hardly had the words left her mouth than shouts were heard.

"Look out, there! Look out, there! Run for you life!"

Mike Kelly looked quickly around.

As he did so, his face became very white.

Coming toward him was a team of horses attached to a heavy truck.

The driver had lost control of them.

Foam was seen on the horses' mouths, and in the quick glance that Mike gave he could see they were maddened with fright.

Mike saw there was no time to be lost, if he wanted to save his own and Katie's life.

He had to act promptly.

Now the maddened horses were almost upon them.

To the right of him was a fence about as tall as he could reach.

This was his only chance.

Seizing Katie around the waist with his left hand, he grasped the fence with the right.

Mike judged the distance carefully.

He saw that if he staid where he was the horses would surly trample over him and Katie.

He also saw that if he seized the fence, and drew himself up a little, he might escape the hoofs of the maddened beasts.

To think with Mike was to act.

Reaching up with his disengaged right hand, he seized the fence and drew himself partly up.

The strain was terrible.

His muscles stood out like whip-cords.

The weight of Katie and the immense amount of strength he had to have to pull himself up at arm's length was telling on him.

He could feel the hot breath of the horses on his cheek.

Katie possessed considerable courage.

She did not move.

She knew she was in Mike's hands, and felt safe.

With a terrible clatter and a snort the horses dashed on.

Mike felt a twinge of pain in his right knee.

It was where the foremost wheel of the heavy truck pressed against it.

One-eighth of an inch nearer the fence and Mike and Katie would have been trampled to death.

When the horses had passed, Mike lowered Katie to the ground, and loosened his hold on the fence; then he drew a long breath.

"That was a very narrow escape, little girl, wasn't it?" he said.

"I shudder to think, Mike, what would have happened to me if you had not been with me," she murmured, as she cast down her eyes.

Katie was very nervous all the way home.

She was brave enough in the face of danger, but now it was past, her nerves gave way and she trembled violently.

When Katie reached home, she told her mother and father of their wonderful escape from the maddened horses.

Mr. and Mrs. Kane listened eagerly.

Mrs. Kane's face paled when Katie told her how nearly she had come to being killed.

As for Mr. Kane, he went up to Mike and put his right hand on his shoulder, at the same time looking him in the eyes.

"Mike, you have done me and mine a great service. How can I repay you?"

"By saying nothing about it, Mr. Kane."

Mike returned home.

Mr. Kane lost no time telling some of his friends of Mike's brave act in saving Katie from death.

Soon the story was known all around town.

When Eddie Carter heard the story, he was pleased.

"Didn't I tell you Mike was a great man?" he asked of Charlie Hurd.

"Yes, and, if he hadn't caught and thrown so much in ball games, he would never have had the strength to lift himself and Katie up on that fence."

Every one agreed with Charlie Hurd that Mike's base-ball playing had given him strength to offset the terrible danger from the maddened horses.

Chapter III. The Paterson Club Accept a Challenge

There had been great rivalry between the Paterson and Newark baseball clubs.

A number of games had been played, in which each had won, and the day was set for a game, which was to decide the championship between the two cities.

Mike had been practicing for a week, so as to get in good form.

Every one knew he was going to catch for the Paterson team, and consequently there was great interest to see him.

The Newark team had been strengthened by a number of good players, and even the Paterson boys, who knew and liked Mike Kelly, said if the home club won it would only be by hard and clever work.

"Do you think our boys will win?" asked Gus Beales of Mike the morning of the game.

"You never can tell anything about a ball game until it is over," said Mike, laughingly.

"That's so. What do you think the chances are?"

"I would not be a member of the Paterson Ball Club, and it's catcher, if I did not think our boys would win."

"That's good enough for me," said Gus, as he walked away.

There was a Newark man in town who wanted to bet five hundred dollars the Newark boys would win, and Gus Beales, who was a good deal of a sport, determined to cover that bet at once.

"Mike Kelly's opinion is good enough for me," he said to himself, as he walked along the street whistling.

It seemed as though all Paterson and Newark were gathered on the ball field that afternoon.

As Mike looked over the immense gathering, numbering nearly twenty thousand people, he said to himself:

"Perhaps this is the beginning of my dream."

Mike's dream was that he was a member of one of the League ball clubs, and its catcher, receiving an immense salary.

"I can almost imagine that I am the lucky man now," he said, as he looked at the grand stand.

Mike had more than one reason for looking over that large crowd of people.

He wanted to see if Katie Kane occupied the seat he told her to.

Sure enough, there was Katie.

She was dressed in honor of the occasion, in light muslin, and had a blue ribbon tied around her neck.

She also wore a white hat with a big blue feather, and Mike thought he never had seen her look so well.

At this time the Paterson and Newark clubs were on the field.

The Paterson uniform was gray, with blue cap.

The Newark boys wore grayish white, and gray caps.

The players looked very well as they sized up in the middle of the field, as the captain of each team tossed for first inning.

It was a beautiful day.

Above, the clouds were white and bluish, and the sun was not hot enough to make ball playing uncomfortable.

There was a slight breeze stirring, which permitted the spectators to witness the game in comfort.

It was a moment of great interest for both clubs.

The captains of each were about to toss.

Captain Jones of the Paterson team held the penny in his hand.

He was about to toss it, when Eddie Carter cried:

"Let Mike Kelly call."

"Yes. Let Mike Kelly call. He's lucky."

"Mike Kelly! Mike Kelly! Mike Kelly!"

"Come here, Mike, you're in demand," cried Captain Jones.

Mike, who was very modest, drew back a little.

His friends had always told him that modest worth would be more valuable to him in later life than a pushing disposition, and he was afraid that if he answered Captain Jones' summons, and came to the front and called the coin as it was tossed in the air, he might make some enemies among those players who were not so popular as he.

"Come, Mike, you are wanted," cried Captain Jones again.

"Yes, let Mike Kelly call the coin! Let Mike Kelly call the coin!"

By this time the whole grand stand was crying Mike's name.

Blushing like a schoolgirl, he approached the crowd where the two captains stood.

Captain Williams, of the Newark Club, wore an anxious expression.

He knew much depended on the toss of the coin.

If the Newark Club was lucky enough to call the coin as it fell, it would have the choice of innings, and in consequence of the beautiful day and the perfect condition of the grounds, the club that took the field first would have last innings.

Both Captain Jones and Captain Williams knew the importance of the first inning.

As Mike advanced toward the two captains, the hubbub in the stand became greater than ever.

"Give us Mike Kelly! He's the one we want!" cried Eddie Carter.

Eddie's cries were taken up by thousands of voices, and again the name of Mike Kelly rose in the air.

As Captain Jones held the coin in his hand ready to toss it, Mike and all the other players gathered about.

"Remember, Mike, to call the coin before it falls," said Captain Williams, of the Newark club.

"Very well," said Mike.

There was a whizzing sound, and the penny went high in the air.

"Tails!"

It was Mike Kelly's voice.

He had decided that tails would win.

But would it?

Quickly the coin descended.

The anxious expression on the faces of the two captains increased.

Which club had won?

"Tails!"

This time it was Captain Jones who spoke.

"We win."

"Hurrah! Hurrah! Hurrah! Mike Kelly has won!"

Again the cry was taken up in the grand stand, and again his name was on every one's lips.

"Well, what will you do?" asked Captain Williams of Captain Jones.

"Take the field, of course. You don't think we are going to the bat, do you?" asked Captain Jones, as he laughed.

The twenty thousand spectators were not silent. The umpire stood at his place.

All the players were on the field.

The great game between Paterson and Newark clubs was about to begin.

Chapter IV. Mike's Great Catch

Captain Jones, of the Paterson team, was also the pitcher.

As Mike Kelly took his position some distance behind the bat, so as to catch the ball on the bound, thousands of eyes watched his every movement.

Eddie Carter, Charlie Hurd, and other of his friends, almost held their breath as the ball left the pitcher's hands.

It was by no means an exciting part of the game, but each had Mike's interest so much at heart, that he did not want to see him make even a slight error.

"One strike — two strikes."

The umpire's voice rang out loud and clear.

Captain Jones was doing good work.

Two strikes had already been called on the batsman, and only one ball.

The batsman would have to hit the next ball, or be thrown out at first base.

As the umpire called two strikes, Mike Kelly walked toward the home-plate, at the same time picking up the catcher's mask.

"See Mike taking the ball off the bat," cried Eddie Carter.

Again the grand stand was silent.

All eyes were on Mike Kelly and Captain Jones.

"Two balls," shouted the umpire.

Pitcher Jones was in bad form, and was getting wild.

Usually Captain Jones was a very clever pitcher, but he was so anxious to win this game against the Newark Club that he overdid himself.

The batsman had asked for a low ball.

Captain Jones straightened his arm.

Whirr! Whirr! went the ball through the air.

It was just right.

The batsman hit at it, but did not hit it.

Carefully judging the ball, Mike Kelly held his hands.

Although it was very strongly pitched, Mike caught it neatly at the same time pulling his mask off, and throwing it aside on the ground.

As he walked back to the bench, the crowd broke into frantic cheers.

Hurrah! Hurrah! for Mike Kelly, the great catcher!"

The Newark Club had failed to score.

It was now the Paterson boys' chance at the bat.

With grim determination pictured on his face, the first striker seized the bat.

The catcher was in position, and all the other players were on the alert.

The Paterson pitcher was also clever, and the three batsmen were put out in one, two, three order.

Mike Kelly had not had a chance at the bat.

The Paterson boys again took the field amid great excitement.

The first inning showed no runs on either side.

The score was the same in the second, third, and fourth innings.

When the Paterson Club went to the bat for the fifth inning, one of the heaviest batters in the club faced the pitcher.

He hit the first ball that came to him, and sent it whirring over into right field. As he was a fast runner, he reached second base in safety.

The pitcher of the Newark Club was getting wild.

He was unlike Captain Jones, who had by this time settled down to a steady game.

Four balls were called on him, and the batsman took his base.

When the next batsman was seen approaching the base, there was more shouting.

"There he is! There he is! There is Mike Kelly, the great catcher!"

Mike Kelly was seen advancing to the plate.

As he neared it, Eddie Carter, his mascot, handed him his favorite bat.

"Thank you, Eddie. I am very much obliged," he whispered.

"Send it over in left field. That's the spot for it," whispered Eddie, in return.

Mike smiled. He liked to see that Eddie Carter took interest in his play.

There were now two men on bases, one on the second and one on third.

It depended on Mike to bring them in.

Every eye was on him. He first thought he would make a sacrifice hit, and bunt the ball half-way to the short stop.

"Take your time, Mike. There is no one out yet," shouted Captain Jones.

Mike did not strike at the first ball, although it was a good one, and the umpire called one strike on him.

The next ball was just right, and Mike gauged it carefully.

Swinging his bat around, he caught the ball on the end.

It sailed upward like a bird, and landed way over the left fielder's head.

It was a wonderful fly, and as the left fielder had come in at the instruction of Captain Williams, because he thought Mike would bunt, he could not run back in time to catch it.

Mike's fly brought in two runs, the man from third base and the man from second base.

Mike was also able to get to second base.

As the two men came running in, the people in the grand stand went crazy with delight.

Men and women rose in their seats, and shouted.

The most enthusiastic among the women threw flowers down on the bench where Mike could gather them up when he came in.

The game was suspended for nearly a minute, while Mike bowed his thanks.

"Play ball!" cried the umpire.

The umpire's words brought the people to their senses.

They knew the game had to proceed, still Mike saw he had made a great hit with the spectators.

The other batsmen were not so fortunate.

The pitcher of the Newark team had steadied himself, and now the balls were put in with regularity and swiftness.

The Paterson boys were again counted out in one, two, three order.

It was now the Newark boys' turn at the bat.

Through errors the Newark Club scored two runs in the sixth inning.

The score was now even.

Throughout the seventh inning no runs were made.

The score was still a tie, being two to two.

"Something must be done," whispered Captain Jones to Mike, as they took the field for the eighth inning.

"Yes, captain, you must not let the boys score this time."

Captain Jones and Mike Kelly saw to it that the Newark boys did not score.

Their battery was almost perfect.

Captain Jones' arms moved up and down like piston-rods.

Mike's work behind the bat was beautiful.

He caught two men out, and put the third man out while stealing second base.

Through about the same kind of errors that had given the Newark Club two runs, the Paterson boys scored one run in the last part of the eighth inning.

The score was three to two.

"I wish Mike Kelly had made that run," said Ned Burns to Charlie Hurd.

"Yes, it would have been a good thing for him. Still he's very popular, isn't he?"

"Yes, and he deserves it, because he's a good fellow and a wonderful catcher."

It was now the last inning, and the score stood three to two.

The Newark boys had made up their minds they must do something desperate to win.

Their three best men were about to come to the bat.

The first batsman was a tall, broad-shouldered man of great strength.

Captain Jones signaled the fielders to get way out in the field, as he was likely to bat over their heads unless they did so.

True to his reputation, the batter did bat over their heads, and placed the ball so well that he got second base.

As Mike Kelly saw the man on second base with none out, his face got very grave.

"Be careful there, captain," he cried to Jones, who was still in the pitcher's box.

"All right, Mike, I will do my best," was the reply.

It was a very critical moment. Mike saw that the batsman would bunt to short stop, and thus try to get the man who was on second base to third.

He motioned the short stop to run in, which he did.

Sure enough, he bunted and the ball fell into the short stop's hands.

With a good throw, he sent it to first.

By this time the man on second attempted to steal third, but, seeing that the man had been put out a first, he attempted to regain second again, and was barely successful.

There was now one man out and one man on second base.

The anxious expression did not leave Mike Kelly's face.

He knew the eyes of every one on the grand stand were on him, and, if he made an error now, he knew it would cost him a great deal of his popularity.

The next batsman knocked a hard grounder to left field.

The left fielder did not field it in time to put the man out.

There were now two men on bases, one on first, the other on third, and only one man out.

The anxious expression on Mike Kelly's face increased.

"I must not let them win this game," he said to himself.

The next batsman was a big, tall, broad-shouldered fellow.

"Look out for this fellow!" cried Captain Jones.

At the same time he made sign with his hand, which was only known to the in-fielders.

The right and left fielders did go some distance farther out, but the in-fielders kept in close.

Captain Jones' sign indicated that the batsman intended to bunt.

Captain Jones was right.

The batsman did bunt, and was neatly thrown out at first base, the man who was on first in the meantime running to second.

"Now is you time," cried Captain Williams to the batter.

All the Newark men were very big and powerful, and the batsman, who was now at the bat, was no different from the rest.

It lay in his power to bring in at least one run and tie the game.

Mike bit his lips as the batter came up to the plate.

His eyes snapped.

He knew this was the time when he must do something.

"I'll die before I'll lose this game," he muttered.

The batsman did not strike at the first ball, and one strike was called on him.

The umpire was very impartial.

The next ball was a good one, and just right.

The batsman hit it with all his might, and it sailed far up in the air.

So high did it go, that, as Eddie Carter said afterward, it looked as if it would disappear in the clouds.

Captain Jones advanced toward him.

Mike Kelly dashed forward.

Both were ready to catch the ball.

In the meantime when the ball was in the air the batsman who was on third base, had run in and scored his run.

The man on second had taken third.

It was an exciting moment for all hands.

The ball was nearly to the ground.

As Captain Jones rushed forward to catch it, he slipped and fell squarely on his face.

The sun had shifted during the afternoon, and was now full in Mike's face.

He saw the accident which had befallen Captain Jones.

He also looked and saw the ball descending.

Would he catch it?

This was the question that ran through the mind of every one on the grand stand.

Whirling quickly about with the sun to his back, Mike extended his left hand.

The ball fell into it, and he clutched it.

The force of the ball knocked him down, but as he fell he held up his left arm.

He had caught the ball, and with the left hand at that.

It was a wonderful catch.

The spectators went wild with excitement.

The batsman who had run in from third base did not count his run.

The score was three to two in favor of the Paterson Club, and as the Paterson Club was the last to go to the bat in the ninth inning they were not required to play anymore.

The Paterson boys had won the game.

"That's the greatest catch I ever saw on the base-ball field," cried Ned Burns.

"Yes, and no one else but Mike Kelly could have made it," said Charlie Hurd.

Eddie Carter was so pleased he rolled over and over on the grass.

He knew Mike's catch would make him famous.

All that evening, and, in fact, for weeks, Mike's famous catch was talked of in every resort where ball cranks and ball players meet.

It was certainly a great catch, especially as Mike had to turn about with his back to the sun, and only had time to extend his left hand.

"I always thought you had a good right hand, but never gave you credit for having such a wonderful left," said Captain Jones, after the game was over.

Mike Kelly was now known as one of the best players in New Jersey.

His popularity was so great it made him many enemies.

Among these was Billy Blake, a player who had formerly belonged to the Paterson Club, but who had been expelled for crookedness.

Billy thought Mike had something to do with his expulsion from the club, and therefore was very sore on him.

"That fellow is becoming too popular," he muttered to his friend, Max Hart, another disappointed ball player.

Max did not like Mike Kelly any better than Billy Blake.

"What can we do to down the fellow Mike Kelly?" asked Blake of Max Hart, the night after Mike's famous catch.

"I have a scheme."

"What is it?"

"I won't tell you now. Meet me to-morrow, and I will let you know all the details."

"Very well, but you won't fool me, will you?"

"No. I hate Mike Kelly as much as you do, and will do everything to down him."

"Good! Good-by, then, until to-morrow."

Mike Kelly was unconscious of his new-made enemies.

Chapter V. Mike in Deadly Peril

Mike now took a vacation for a couple of weeks.

His employers thought so much of him as a ball player, that they thought if they gave him a couple of weeks to practice in he would improve wonderfully.

They were right.

Mike practiced at the grounds every day with Charlie Hurd, Ned Burns, and other of his friends.

Eddie Carter always joined them in the afternoon.

One day, when Mike was practicing, Eddie came running up to him.

"I have a note for you," he said.

"What is it?" asked the catcher, eagerly.

Mike thought the note might be from Katie Kane.

As he read the signature, he was disappointed.

The note was not from Katie Kane.

It was in a man's handwriting, and asked him if he would make a balloon ascension that afternoon.

"How would you like to see me go up in a balloon, boys?" Mike said.

"First rate," said Ned Burns. "Do you think you have wind enough?"

"I guess so."

"You bet he has," broke in Charlie Hurd. "If the balloon lacks gas, Mike will supply it. Eh, boys?"

"No, I can't stand for that," said Ned. "Mike Kelly is no wind-bag," at which sally all hands laughed.

"That's right. I was only kidding you," said Charlie Hurd.

It was arranged that the balloon ascension should occur in a big, open space of ground.

No one knew who the balloon man was, but as he was to give a free ascension that afternoon a great crowd naturally gathered.

He was a big fellow, and wore a heavy black beard.

Eddie Carter thought he had seen the balloon man's eyes before.

"I don't like the looks of that fellow, Mike," Eddie said, "and, if I were you, I wouldn't go up in the balloon with him."

"Never fear about me, Eddie. I am all right."

As Mike spoke, he smiled.

He knew Eddie was his friend, and that he advised for the best, but he laughed at the boy's fears.

It was agreed that only Mike and the balloon man should ascend.

The time was nearly up, and the men were preparing to let the balloon go.

"Get in the basket," said the balloon man, in a voice Eddie Carter was sure he had heard before.

Again he pulled Mike by the sleeve, and whispered to him.

Still Mike refused to listen to his fears.

"Why shouldn't I go?" he asked. "I have never been up in a balloon, and this is a new experience for me."

A few minutes later, the superintendent, who was on the ground, shouted:

"Are you ready, boys?"

"Yes," cried the balloon man.

"Let her go!" cried Mike.

Each of the five men, who were stationed at the ropes, took out a sharp jackknife.

With one stroke they severed the ropes binding the balloon.

As it shot upward, Mike's companion threw out two bags of sand.

This increased the speed, and in less than a minute it was five hundred feet above the earth.

Still another and another bag of sand was dropped out, and the balloon ascended higher and higher.

Mike was a little frightened.

He could not distinguish the faces of his friends on the ground below, and it was with difficulty that he could tell the differences between the houses below him.

"What's the matter with you, my friend?" he cried. "Do you want to take us above the clouds?"

As Mike looked at the balloon man, he started.

His whole expression had changed.

His eyes now had taken on an expression of deadly hatred.

"Yes, I want to take you up into the clouds," he muttered, as he threw out another bag of sand.

As he spoke, he came over to where Mike was sitting and looked him in the eye.

Mike shrank back into the corner of the basket, at the same time saying: "Who are you?"

"Do you want to know who I am, Mike Kelly?"

"Yes. Who are you? Speak!"

"I am your enemy."

"My enemy?"

"Yes, your enemy."

"Your name?"

"Billy Blake."

As Billy spoke, Mike started.

"What do you mean by bringing me up in this balloon?"

"I mean your death!"

It was an exciting moment.

The two men eyed each other.

Billy slowly backed to where the sand-bags were lying, and, seizing three of them, threw them overboard.

The balloon shot up with lightning-like rapidity.

Mike felt the air becoming colder.

He saw that he had to do something, and at once, or the balloon would be so far into the clouds that he would freeze to death.

"Open that valve, you villain!" cried Mike, as he started to pull open the safety-valve himself.

As he spoke, Billy Blake laughed fiendishly.

"I saw to that valve long before I left the earth, Mike Kelly," he said, as a terrible expression came over his face. "That valve is not in working order."

"Do you mean to say there is no way to make this balloon descend?" said Mike, as he advanced toward Billy.

"Yes; you will meet you death in the clouds, Mike Kelly."

"But how about you, Billy Blake?"

"I am willing to die, if I know you will die, too," and as he spoke the villain uttered a terrible oath.

Neither spoke for a moment.

In the meantime the balloon was ascending with great speed farther and farther up into the clouds.

Mike felt his fingers becoming colder and colder.

He must do something at once, he thought. Billy Blake evidently read Mike's thoughts.

He said, as he pulled off his heave black beard, and showed Mike the features of the ball player he knew so well:

"Mike Kelly, your hour has come. I have you now."

"Not yet."

Mike still kept his eyes on Billy.

His hand was in his pocket.

He grasped his pocket-knife, and opened it.

It was small, but very sharp.

He had been considering a plan of action.

As he uttered the words: "Not yet," he sprang over the car, and seized one of the ropes leading up into the balloon.

Mike, who was an athlete, climbed hand over hand until he had reached a position far above Billy Blake's head.

Entwining his feet in the ropes, and holding on with his left hand, with his right Mike took the knife from his pocked.

Plunging it into the balloon, he made a big hole, from which the gas issued in torrents.

As he cut the balloon, he turned his head, else he would have been suffocated by the escaping gas.

The balloon came to a sudden stop, and then began to descent but not so quickly as it had ascended.

As Billy Blake saw what he had done, he uttered another oath, and cried: "Foiled again."

He could not reach Mike Kelly to do him an injury.

Mike's position was a perilous one.

He was very strong, and he held on tightly.

He knew his life depended upon it.

The balloon was now descending faster than before.

As each hundred yards was passed its momentum increased, and Mike knew unless something unforeseen occurred his life was saved.

Mike could distinguish the houses now, and knew he was not far from the ground.

When Billy Blake saw his plan to injure Mike had failed, he looked around for some means to escape.

He had made up his mind to jump at the first opportunity.

He knew if Mike reached the ground, he would have him arrested for attempting his life.

When nearly to the ground the balloon caught in a big chimney.

Mike's position was again perilous, but a little wind drew it from the chimney, and it sailed slowly toward the ground.

As it neared the roof of a house, Billy Blake threw out an anchor.

This caught in the side of a house, and permitted him to steady the balloon for an instant.

Taking advantage of the opportunity, he sprang on the roof, at the same time pushing the balloon away from him.

The last words Mike Kelly heard, as the balloon descended to the ground — a distance of a hundred feet — were these:

"You have foiled me this time, Mike Kelly, but I will yet have your life."

"Oh, how that man must hate me!" said Mike to himself.

When the balloon reached the ground, Mike stepped from the care in safety.

He found, by making inquiries, the balloon had sailed a distance of over ten miles, and he was in the center of a farming country.

Mike told his story to the people whom he met, and after an hour's wait at a railroad station near by he took the next train for Paterson.

It was a startling experience for him, and one he would never forget.

He told himself he would spare no means to bring Billy Blake to justice.

It was late that night when he returned home, and he went direct to bed, vowing if Billy ever crossed his path again it would go hard with him.

Chapter VI. Mike's Plans for the Future

When Mike Kelly told of his experiences of the afternoon before, when Billy Blake tried to kill him in the balloon, his friends were indignant.

Eddie Carter, who was more attached to Mike than ever, said if he met Billy Blake he would give him in charge of an officer.

"Oh, the villain!" said the little fellow, as he clenched his fist. "I wish I had been there, that's all."

Mike and his friends laughed at Eddie's enthusiasm.

They all knew he was devoted to Mike, but as he was such a little fellow, and Mike was so big, they had to smile when Eddie said that the villain, Billy Blake, would not have done as he did had he been present.

In a week or so the balloon incident, in which Mike came so near losing his life, was forgotten.

Mike made a search for Billy Blake, but found that he had left town.

He did not worry any more about the matter, and said to himself that he was well rid of him forever.

He did not know, however, the vindictive character of Billy Blake.

He also did not know that at that very moment Billy was in New York plotting against his life.

Mike continued to practice every time he could get the chance.

His name was well-known in all the resorts where base-ball men gathered.

At Nick Engel's, in Twenty-seventh street, New York, he was a frequent visitor.

Every one was glad to see him.

His popularity did not turn his head, though, and he was as modest and unassuming as ever.

One afternoon he was catching to Captain Jones' pitching, when Charlie Hurd walked up.

Charlie was accompanied by Ned Burns.

Charlie watched Mike catch for some moments, and then took him aside.

"Say, Mike, I want to tell you something."

"What is it, Charlie?"

"I want to say that you are much too good for this city. You ought to join another and bigger club."

"How do you know but I will some day?"

"Do you think of doing so?" asked the other, eagerly.

"Strange things have happened, Charlie. I received half an offer from —"

At this moment Mike's attention was attracted to Eddie Carter, his mascot, who was running toward him.

Eddie held an envelope in his hand.

"Ah! What if it should be it?" said Mike, half to himself, but loud enough for Charlie to hear.

"I — I saw a messenger boy with this in his hand," said Eddie, who was out of breath, "and I took it from him, and ran."

Mike snatched the envlepoe out of Eddie's hands, and read its contents.

As he did so, he smiled.

As he handed the telegram to Charlie Hurd, he said:

"It has come sooner than I thought, Charlie."

Charlie's eyes opened wide, as he, too, read the telegram.

"Why, boy, you are in luck," was all he said, as he patted Mike on the back.

This is a copy of the telegram that caused Mike and Charlie so much pleasure:

> "To Mike Kelly, Paterson, N. J. — See me at the St. James Hotel in New York, Tuesday, at 3 o'clock in regard to signing.
>
> "President of the Chicago Base-Ball Club."

The telegram was dated Chicago.

Charlie passed it to Eddie Carter, who looked surprised.

Eddie could not restrain his joy.

He jumped up and down, and cried at the top of his voice:

"Mike Kelly's got there. I told you Mike Kelly would get there."

While Eddie was jumping up and down, the messenger boy from whom he had taken the telegram ran up.

He, too, was out of breath.

"Say, young feller, where is me dispatch?"

Eddie did not answer him.

He continued to cry that Mike Kelly had got there.

"Look'ee here, me friend," said the messenger again, "if yer don't giv' me me dispatch I'll smash yer in de snoot."

This threat caused Eddie to stop for a moment.

"You'll smash who?" and in a second the two boys were rolling over and over on the grass.

When Mike could recover from the fit of laughter into which the actions of the messenger had thrown him, he separated the two boys, at the same time saying: "Here, this won't do, my lad. I have your telegram."

As the messenger looked up, and say who the speaker was, he gasped: "Is that you, Mr. Kelly?"

In an instant the boy became very obedient and willing.

After Mike had signed the book, the messenger ran away, but not until he had shaken his fist at Eddie Carter.

"And you are really going to become a professional?" asked Eddie, who could hardly believe the telegram which Mike held in his hand.

"I will, if I can."

"Good boy, that's the way to talk," said Charlie Hurd.

Soon every one in Paterson knew that Mike Kelly intended to turn professional.

He was greeted on every hand by such expressions as these:

"Ah! there, Mike, are you going to catch for the Chicago team?"

"Hello! Mr. Professional Catcher!"

"Ah! there, Michael!"

These and similar remarks pleased Mike Kelly. "If I am only as popular as a professional, I'll be a lucky man," he said to himself.

As the day for the meeting with the President of the Chicago Base-Ball Club drew near, Mike grew nervous.

He was anxious to take up ball playing as a living, but was not certain as to whether he and the ball magnate could come to terms.

"I'll know to-morrow," he said, as he went to bed.

The following afternoon he was to meet the President of the Chicago Club.

That night Mike again had a dream in which he saw himself catching ball to an audience of twenty thousand people.

Chaper VII. Mike Becomes a Professional

Toward daylight Mike Kelly awoke.

With a bound, he jumped out of bed, and was soon in his clothes.

While waiting for his breakfast, he went to the ball-ground and practiced high throwing all alone.

While he was thus engaged, Eddie Carter came up.

"Hello! Mike, you're out early, aren't you?"

"Yes, I like the early morning air."

"This is the day you meet the President of the Chicago Club, isn't it?"

"Yes."

"When do you leave for New York?"

"At nine o'clock. Do you want to go?"

"Will you take me, really?"

"Why, certainly. Aren't you my mascot?"

Eddie was very happy when Mike Kelly told him he could go to New York with him.

He had only been to New York once, and then when he was very young.

"Meet me at the depot, Eddie," said Mike, as he put on his coat and walked in the direction of his home.

Eddie was early at the depot.

It was generally known in Paterson that Mike intended leaving town that morning with a view to signing with the Chicago Club.

In consequence there was a great gathering of his friends to see him off.

Charlie Hurd and Ned Burns were there, and Captain Jones arrived just before the train left.

Each wished him good luck, and as the train drew out of the depot cheers rent the air.

"Hurrah for Mike Kelly!" cried Charlie Hurd.

As the train passed out of sight, there was a quiver in Mike's voice as he spoke to Eddie Carter.

"They're very kind to me. I shall be sorry to leave all my old friends in Paterson."

"Yes, and they will be sorry to lose you."

The trip to New York was uneventful.

Mike and Eddie were a little ahead of time, and had to wait at the St. James Hotel for the President of the Chicago Club.

He soon came in, and greeted the two pleasantly.

"Is this a ball player, too?" he asked, as he looked at Eddie Carter.

"No; but he hopes to be some day, don't you, Eddie?"

Eddie nodded.

"This is my mascot, Eddie Carter."

"That's right, Mr. Kelly. It doen't hurt a ball-player to have a mascot."

"Yes, if he's lucky."

Eddie Carter looked injured, but did not speak.

Mike saw the expression on his face, and added:

"Eddie's the luckiest boy on earth," which made the little fellow smile.

After a few minutes' talk on the prospect of the base-ball season, the President of the Chicago Club said:

"I suppose you know why I telegraphed you to meet me?"

"I have some idea."

"I want you to join my club."

Mike's eyes flashed.

"In what position am I to play?"

"Catcher, of course."

The two soon came to terms, and before Mike Kelly left the St. James Hotel he had signed an agreement to play with the Chicago League Base-Ball Club.

"Well?" said Eddie Carter, after they had bidden good-by to the president and were on their way to Paterson again.

"Well?" echoed Mike, as he smiled.

"You're a professional ball player now for fair."

"Yes; do you think I will make a good one?"

"Out of sight."

"Will you go with me to Chicago?"

Eddie was not surprised at anything Mike might do or say.

He said he would go anywhere Mike did, and that settled the matter.

Mike was to leave for Chicago in two days.

He bade good-by to all his old friends, who said they would give him a great send off.

He had some trouble securing Mr. Carter's consent to let Eddie go, but after some coaxing that gentleman said:

"I know you'll take good care of Eddie, Mike."

"That I will, Mr. Carter."

And so it was arranged that Eddie should accompany Mike to Chicago.

When Mike reached the depot on the morning of his departure, he was surprised at the large crowd waiting to see him off. As he appeared, a band began to play the opening strains of "See the Conquering Hero Comes!"

"Ah! My friends have not forgotten me," he said to himself, as he grasped the hands of the boys.

"One would think Mike was the President of the United States," said Charlie Hurd.

"Yes, he is quite an important citizen to-day," said Ned Burns.

The time came when Mike had to say the last good-by.

The band played the air of Harry Kennedy's beautiful song, "Say Au Revoir, But Not Good-By," the whistle blew, and Mike Kelly left behind him the old life to begin the new.

He and Eddie did not remain long in New York. They were anxious to get to Chicago.

Mike's reputation as a catcher had preceded him.

All the Chicago players had heard of his wonderful work behind the bat, and each gave him a great welcome.

"Eddie, I play my first game with the Chicago team to-morrow," said Mike, four days after he had reached that city."

"Yes; and you will have to do your prettiest."

"I'll do all I know how," said Mike, as he smiled.

Chapter VIII. Mike's Firest Professional Game

The next day was a very important one for Mike Kelly.

He was to make his first appearance on the professional ball-field with the famous Chicago team.

He and Eddie were up bright and early.

Mike practiced in the morning, and returned to the Palmer House for dinner, after which he took a nap.

He wanted to be in good shape for the afternoon game.

The Chicago Club was scheduled to play the Cleveland Club.

There was great rivalry between the two clubs and every one said Mike had the chance of his life to make himself famous.

Mike knew the report of the game would be telegraphed to Paterson, and he was anxious to make a good showing, if only for their sake.

Eddie carefully brushed his street clothes, and when Mike left the Palmer Huse for the ball-grounds he looked a fashion-plate.

During his short stay in Chicago, Mike had made many friends.

They were present to encourage him.

When he put on his base-ball suit, and was ready to go on the field, a telegram was put into his hands. It was from Katie Kane.

In it she said she hoped Mike would make a success.

"Dear little girl, how thoughtful she is," Mike said softly to himself, as he opened half a dozen other telegrams.

These were from friends in Paterson and New York, all wishing him good luck and encouraging him.

As Mike appeared there was a faint cheer.

"They'll cheer him for fair before the game if over," said Eddie Carter, who carried Mike's favorite bats.

Most of the work in the early innings was done by the fielders.

Mike occasionally threw to second, and put out a man.

His work was entirely satisfactory up to this time, but he had not done anything brilliant.

"Watch him, that's all," said Eddie Carter to another boy, who sat on the bench with him.

There were fully ten thousand people in the grand stand, and Mike was wishing for a chance to show what he could do.

The chance came in the eighth inning.

The score was: Chicago, 3; Ceveland, 2.

Cleveland was at the bat.

No one was out.

There was one man on first and another on second.

"Two strikes," shouted the umpire.

The captain of the Cleveland team smiled.

As there were two men on bases and none out, he thought his club was reasonably sure of at least one run.

What if the batter did strike out?

What difference did it make?

These thoughts ran through the head of the Cleveland captain.

"Three strikes!"

Again the umpire's voice rang out.

Hardly had the words left his mouth before Mike Kelly's arms shot back.

He had caught the ball, thus putting the striker out.

He had had his eyes on second base before the umpire called:

"Three strikes."

The player on that base was about to steal.

As the ball left the pitcher's hand, he ran.

The ball was a swift one, true as a die.

Hardly had the ball reached Mike's hands than it left them again, this time to be thrown to third base.

The third baseman was alert.

He caught it, and, running forward, touched the runner from second, who was going so fast he could not stop.

Quick as a flash the third baseman threw the ball to the second baseman, who was standing on the bag.

When the Cleveland man on first saw Mike throw to third he ran.

Had it not been for the third baseman's quickness he might have reached second.

The ball beat him, however, by a fraction.

The third baseman in his excitement threw it low.

Bending down, the second baseman caught the ball and touched the Cleveland man as he slid.

"Three men out," shouted the umpire.

It was a triple play.

For an instant the spectators were paralyzed.

When they recovered from their astonishment every one stood on his or her feet.

Wild cheering rent the air.

A triple play!

It was something unusual.

Soon the spectators understood that the three men were put out owing to the quickness and good judgment of Mike Kelly.

"Hurrah for Mike Kelly!"

"Hurrah! Hurrah! Hurrah!"

For some minutes the excitement ran so high that the game could not proceed.

The umpire cried:

"Batter up," time and time again, but no batter came.

The Chicago players themselves had caught the enthusiasm and were also shouting.

When Mike Kelly's name was shouted, he pointed to the third and second basemen.

Mike was modest.

He did not want to take all the credit for his wonderful play.

Still the crowd cheered him.

By Mike Kelly's triple play, assisted by the third and second basemen, the score remained the same as before: Chicago, 3; Cleveland, 2.

The Cleveland men took the field with glum faces.

Each member of the team thought when he saw two men on bases and none out that the score would at least be tied.

"Come, come, batter up," shouted the umpire, who was becoming impatient.

By this time the batter had taken his place, and the cheering had ceased.

The balance of the game was not remarkable in point of play.

Neither side scored, and thus the Chicago Club won by a score of 3 to 2.

All the players congratulated Mike on his wonderful play, and the next day the Chicago papers gave him credit for winning the game.

Mike was very happy.

Eddie Carter was so tickled that he ran about telling everybody what a great catcher Mike Kelly was.

"Hurrah! Mike, you're just in time."

Mike Kelly received these words by telegraph the next morning.

The telegram was signed:

"Your old pal, Charlie Hurd."

"I wish Charlie was here now," Mike said, as he put the telegram in his pocket.

All that week Mike continued his success.

Chicago base-ball experts said his coming with the team had greatly increased its strength.

Throughout the country, too, he got a great reception.

During the season he increased his popularity to such an extent that his presence in the nine was received with great enthusiasm.

It was noticed the days on which he played the attendance was larger than usual.

Eddie Carter traveled with him everywhere. When asked what the attraction between them was, Mike asid: “Eddie is my mascot. I wouldn't be lucky unless he was with me.”

The latter part of the season showed Mike's popularity to be greater than ever before. A number of clubs signified their intentions of bidding for his services.

The President of the Chicago Club, on hearing of these offers, said: “If any club wants Mike Kelly it will have to pay dearly for him.”

The end of the season found Mike at the head of the catcher's class. His record was excellent, and his friends in Paterson said there was no limit to which he might not rise. “He's the best base-ball player in the world, and I'm his mascot; see?” said Eddie Carter, when he spoke of Mike Kelly.

Chapter IX. “King Kelly to the Bat”

“Who plays de New Yorks ter-day, Snookey?” asked one newsboy of another on Park row, New York.

“De Chicagos.”

“Is dat so.”

“Sure, an' it's meself won't miss de game.”

“Naw? Will yez stake me ter a dime?”

“Wot fur?”

“To go ter de ball game wid. If I gits up dere I kin see de game in a hole in de fence.”

“Take a walk. Wot do yer think I am? A Wanderbilt?”

“Mike Kelly plays ter day.”

“Duz he? Den I'm off,” and , as the boy with money spoke, he ran to the elevated road, where he took the train for the Polo Grounds.

The other boy looked at his disappearing figure, and said to himself:

“Dat kid's too gay. I'll do him up when I gets der chance.”

Mike Kelly's name was as well known in New York as in Chicago.

Although with a rival team, he was very popular with New Yorkers, and an announcement that he was to play always attracted a great crowd to the Polo Grounds.

On this particular day there were ten thousand spectators waiting to see the struggle between the New Yorks and the Chicagos.

Each had won a game, and this was to see which would win the odd one of the series.

The nerves of each player on the two nines were at high tension.

The Chicago boys knew their friends expected them to give a good account of themselves.

As to the members of the New York team, they also knew that the eyes of every lover of base-ball in the Metropolis were upon them.

"We'll have to lick 'em to-day or get licked ourselves," said one New York player to another.

He meant if the New Yorks did not win, that the players on the team would get a beating at the hands of the indignant directors of the club.

The other laughed at the remark, and passed into the dressing-room.

"Ah! there, Mike," said a member of the Chicagos. "Will we be on the hog train to-day?"

"I hope not."

Mike and the speaker had their uniforms on, and were walking in the direction of the grand stand.

"Ah! there he is. There's Mike Kelly!"

The cry came from a boy on the bleaching boards.

"Yes, dere's de great catcher."

The cry was taken up by the grand stand.

"Kelly! Kelly! Kelly!"

"Hello! Mike!"

"Ah! there, Mike."

"There's the king of base-ball players."

"King Kelly. Hurrah! Hurrah! Hurrah!"

"They call me king now, eh?" said Mike to himself. "That's good, I'm growing a little every day."

The cheering ceased, and the game began.

Up to the sixth inning neither side made a run.

Kelly's catching was much admired.

He had made no errors up to this time.

In the sixth inning there were two men out and one on third base.

It was Mike Kelly's turn at the bat.

"King Kelly to the bat," cried a friend of Mike's in the grand stand. "He'll bring the run in."

As Eddie Carter heard Mike called "King Kelly," he said to himself:

"That name will stick to Mike."

Mike walked to the bat with determination in his eyes.

He knew all eyes were on him.

He could not make a sacrifice hit; for, if he did, he would be thrown out at first base.

This would make three out, with one man left on base.

He either had to knock a fly over the right or left fielder's head, or a safe grounder which would permit him to reach first and bring the man on third in.

One strike was called on Mike, as he looked for a weak spot in the New York field.

He saw the spot.

The chance came with the next ball.

It just suited Mike.

Striking it plumb in the center, he sent it with terrible force between the first base and the first baseman.

He could not have judged the spot more carefully.

There was no first baseman to receive it.

It was left to the fielder to throw the ball to first.

When he picked it up, and threw it to first, Mike Kelly was already there, and the run had already been scored.

Again, Mike Kelly had won the day.

How the grand stand cheered!

How men and boys stood on their seats, and cried for King Kelly!

It was a great moment for Mike.

When play was resumed, the next striker was caught out.

But this did not matter.

There were no more runs made by either club, and King Kelly, as he was now called, had won the game.

Although the majority of those present wanted to see the New Yorks win, they could not help applaud Mike Kelly's clever hit.

When the game was over, men ran forward to carry Mike to his dressing-room.

But Mike anticipated them.

Calling to Eddie to follow, he reached his dressing-room, and was soon in his street clothes.

Everywhere he went that night, to the music halls or to the hotels, Mike was congratulated on his clever hit.

"The New York team ought to get King Kelly," said a base-ball crank, in the corridor of the Hoffman House that night.

"Perhaps the king will come to New York next season," was the reply.

"Stranger things have happened."

When questioned as to whether he would like to play with the New Yorks next season, Mike said:

"I'll answer that question when I am asked."

Mike was pleased at his success.

But one thing troubled him.

The day before he had come face to face with his enemy, Billy Blake.

When Billy saw Mike, he sneaked away in the crowd on Broadway.

The sight of Billy Blake was offset by a letter he received that morning from Katie Kane.

"I glory in your success," Katie wrote.

"Of course she does, the dear little girl," said Mike.

Chapter X. Billy Blake's Threat

Mike Kelly was troubled the next day by the thought that Billy Blake would leave no stone unturned to do him an injury.

"I wonder if Max Hart is with him?" he asked himself.

So quickly did Billy disappear in the crowd that Mike did not have a chance to see whether or not he had a companion.

Mike's friends could not do too much for him.

Everywhere he went he was received with every evidence of approval.

His playing of the day before had made his name a familiar one to every lover of base-ball.

Late in the afternoon of the following day, he entered the *cafe* of the Hoffman House.

Billy Edwards was entertaining a group at one table, while at the others were well known men-about-town and base-ball cranks.

"Hello, Mike! take a seat!" was Billy Edwards' cheerful greeting.

"Thanks, Billy."

Mike was introduced to those gentlemen he did not know.

The talk naturally turned to base-ball and Mike's fine catching of the day before.

While he talked, Mike glanced at a table opposite.

As he did so, he started.

He saw Billy Blake watching him.

He had discarded his false beard.

By his side sat Max Hart.

"Ha! My enemies are near," he said. "I wonder if they intend doing me any harm?"

Mike could see that Billy's eyes looked like the eyes of a snake.

As Mike watched his enemy he rose, and with Max Hart left the *cafe*.

"That fellow's a bad egg," Mike said, and then Billy Blake slipped from his mind in the conversation of his friends.

With no fear of danger Mike left the party and started in the direction of Sixth avenue.

He had his head down. He was in a deep thought.

When half-way between Sixth avenue and Broadway, he ran into a man, who, with an oath, was about to pass on.

The two were under a lamp-post.

"Billy Blake!"

"Mike Kelly!"

Both men spoke at once.

"Ha! Ha! We meet again, Mike Kelly," said Billy Blake, as he looked at the ball player.

"Yes, villain! we meet again. I should give you in charge of the police for attempting my life."

"You forget, Mike Kelly, we are not in Paterson now," and, as he spoke, Billy sneered.

"Yes; but I could get justice here as well."

"Why don't you start in?"

"Because I want nothing to do with you, and—"

Mike did not finish the sentence.

Before he could, Billy hissed between his teeth:

"And — well, go on. Do you want me to tell you something?"

Mike smiled, but did not speak.

He did not seem to care for what Billy had to say, but the villain continued: "I want to say this to you. Before a week you will no longer be a member of the Chicago Club."

Mike smiled again.

Billy Blake's words amused him.

"Who will cause my discharge?" he said, this time smiling more than before.

"I will."

Billy Blake's words made Mike laugh outright.

"You? That's a good joke."

"Yes; you may laugh, Mike Kelly, but remember Billy Blake has said it."

As Billy Blake spoke, he backed away from Mike and disappeared in the area-way of an adjacent house.

Mike looked back from time to time to see that Billy did not attempt any foul play.

He knew he was treacherous.

His threat troubled him for a few minutes, but finally he dismissed it, and the man who made it, from his mind.

"Pshaw! What harm can he do me?" he said to himself as he walked in the direction of his hotel.

Chapter XI. Mike Kelly, the Ten-Thousand-Dollar Ball Player

The next afternoon Mike Kelly repeated his former triumph.

He received the applause of the crowd, and Eddie Carter went wild with joy.

Eddie often wrote home to Paterson, telling Mike's friends how popular he was.

It was toward the end of the season.

Each club was striving to gain the championship.

There was great rivalry between them, and all the cities interested were encouraging their teams to do their utmost.

"We would do better, if we had Mike Kelly," said a Boston base-ball crank, who was on a visit to New York, and who saw Mike catch for the Chicago Club.

"Who knows? We may have him next season," said his companion, who was interested.

The base-ball season had no sooner ended than the bidding commenced for Mike Kelly's services.

As he had signed with the Chicago Club, and it refused to release him, other clubs would have to bid large sums of money to secure his release.

The Boston Club was early in the field as a bidder. Its managers had watched Mike's playing very carefully the season before, and were determined to secure him, if possible.

As other clubs were anxious to include Mike in their nine, the bidding increased.

"Whew! Mike, but you *are* popular," said Charlie Hurd to the famous catcher, one day, when he was paying a visit to his old friends in Paterson.

"Why?"

"Here's an offer from a Western club of five thousand dollars for your release."

"Is that so?"

"Yes, and I hear the Boston Club will give even more than that to secure you."

Mike was well pleased. He was glad to know his services were in such demand.

Mike's days were pleasantly passed among his old friends. He saw Katie Kane every day. The two young people took long drives, and were very happy in each other's society.

Mike delivered Eddie Carter safely into his father's hands. As he did so, he exacted a promise for Mr. Carter that he would let Eddie go with him the following season.

During this time when the clubs were arranging for the next season, the base-ball magnates were busy bidding for Mike's services.

He had made such a success with the Chicago Club that its managers did not want to let him go.

The figures got higher and higher as the days went by.

Some Western club offered seven thousand five hundred dollars for Mike's release.

"Where will it end?" asked Mr. Carter of Eddie, one morning when he read of the offer.

"I don't know. Do you know what I think Mike is worth?"

"No."

"If I had my way, I would give him a hundred thousand dollars."

"That's because he is your friend, and has been kind to you."

"No; but because he is the best ball player in America."

Mike watched the bidding for his services with great interest.

He knew every raise made him more valuable as a base-ball star.

"Hurrah! Hurrah!" shouted Eddie Carter, as he ran down the main street of Paterson, waving a paper in his hand.

He had gone but a couple of blocks when he met Mike Kelly.

He was as well dressed and as good-natured as usual.

"What is it, Eddie?" asked Mike.

"Oh! I'm so happy," and, as the boy spoke, he turned a somersault.

"What is it? Tell me, quick?"

Mike was becoming impatient.

Eddie stopped short in his gymnastic exercise, and held the paper out to Mike.

As he read the first column, his face got very grave, and he gasped:

"Impossible!"

As he read on, his eyes got larger and larger.

Before he finished, Eddie said:

"Didn't I tell you, Mike? Hurrah! Hurrah! for Mike Kelly!"

Mike had just read that the Boston Club had offered ten thousand dollars for his release.

He whistled long and loud.

"Well, well, well."

Eddie was watching the expression on his face.

"Didn't I tell you?" he cried again and again.

Every base-ball crank in Paterson knew of the big offer for Mike's services.

He went to New York that day, and visited Nick Engel's.

He was received with great enthusiasm.

As he walked along Broadway, he frequently heard his name mentioned.

The managers of the Chicago and Boston clubs met.

After some discussion the Chicago managers agreed to accept ten thousand dollars for Mike Kelly's release.

Mike soon learned of their decision, and was not displeased.

He liked Boston and her people.

When the announcement that the famous catcher would go to Boston was telegraphed to the Bean City, great crowds gathered about the bulletin boards.

"Hurrah! for the ten-thousand-dollar beauty!" cried a base-ball crank.

The cry was taken up and repeated a dozen times.

"Hurrah for King Kelly!"

Mike will never forget his first visit to Boston.

He was met at the train, and escorted to his hotel in a four-in-hand.

The winter months soon passed, and the spring, with its base-ball season, came.

Mike was practicing daily with the Boston team.

He had greatly improved in his work, and was looking forward to the time when the Boston and Chicago teams should meet in the field.

"I wonder what the boys in Chicago will say when they see me catching for the Bostons?" Mike asked Eddie Carter.

"They will say you are out of sight."

Mike did very well during the first few games of the season.

He was waiting, though, until the Bostons went to Chicago, as he knew that a great reception awaited him in that city.

Chapter XII. Mike in Great Form

It had been arranged that the Boston team should visit Chicago after playing a few games at home.

Mike had long looked forward to seeing the many friends he had made in Chicago.

"I must be in my best form when we meet the Chicago boys," he told Eddie Carter, as together with the team he was traveling on the train for the Western city.

"You bet you will. It won't do to let your old friends beat you too many games."

Mike was unusually silent all the journey.

When he was not thinking of his friends in Paterson he was figuring out the chances of the Boston Club winning against their Western rivals.

As Mike anticipated, his reception in the city where he had played the season previous was all that was cordial.

The fact that the Boston boys were on their way had been telegraphed ahead.

As in Boston, the station was crowded.

The first words Mike heard, were:

"Where is the king?""

"Where is King Kelly?"

In an instant he was surrounded by public officials and base-ball men.

Pat Powers, one of Mike's oldest friends, was in the crowd.

"Hello! Mike!"

"Hello! Pat! how's Chicago?"

"Glad to see you, old man."

"That's nice."

All that evening and until Eddie warned Mike it was time to go to bed, the reception went on.

As Mike laid his head on his pillow, he said softly to himself:

"There are worse situations in life than that of a successful ball player."

The first game between the Bostons and the Chicagos was to come off the next day.

Mike arose early, and went to the ball grounds.

He wanted to practice.

He was a little stale on the diamond, as he had not played on it since the previous autumn.

When the afternoon came, and great crowds poured in at the gates, Mike was in the best of condition and spirits.

Eddie Carter had brushed and cleaned his uniform, and selected his favorite bats.

It would not be Eddie's fault, Mike thought, if the Bostons did not win the game.

If Mike had thought his previous receptions at the hands of the Chicago people were flattering, he did not know what his friends were capable of.

No sooner did he appear than the people on the grand stand went into a frenzy of excitement.

Hats were thrown into the air, and men seized each other about the waists, and shouted like mad.

"It's a great reception for Mike," said Pat Powers to a gentleman connected with the Chicago Club.

"Yes, and he deserves it."

The reception was remarkable, because Mike was playing on a rival team.

The umpire called the game, and the Bostons took the field.

This was Mike's chance to show his form.

His catching was remarkable.

The batsmen went out one after another.

The Bostons made one run.

"Now, Mike, remember — no runs," said the captain of the Boston team, as the club again took the field.

"All right, I'll attend to that end of it."

Mike was true to his word.

His catching was perfect.

"Down, down to second," cried the captain of the Chicago team to a batsman, who succeeded in reaching first.

The ball had just reached Mike's hands.

With a quick throw, he sent the ball to second.

The baseman was on the plate.

The runner did not beat the ball.

The baseman touched him, and cried:

"Judgment?"

"Out;" cried the umpire.

Mike's clever throw was applauded.

Throughout the nine innings Mike Kelly's work behind the bat continued.

Assisted by the pitcher, he put out man after man.

When the game was finished, the score stood: Boston, 1; Chicago, 0.

Mike's superior play had won the game for the bean-eaters.

Although Chicago people wanted to see the home team win, they did not neglect to applaud Mike.

He was such a favorite that it was only with difficulty that he could get to his dressing-room, so great was the crowd.

"You did nobly, Mike," said Pat Powers, half an hour later. "You are an honor to the Boston Club."

"Thanks, Pat. I appreciate your kindness."

Mike was modest and unassuming, yet he would not have been a ball player if he did not appreciate the many acts of favor shown him.

Chapter XIII. "Casey at the Bat"

Mike had become so popular that he determined to take his friends' advice and go on the stage after the close of the base-ball season.

He had received an offer from Manager Krause, of the Imperial Music Hall, New York city.

"Does he pay you ten thousand dollars?" asked Charlie Hurd of Mike, one day as they walked up Broadway.

"Not quite, but near it," and the two friends laughed heartily.

When the season closed, Mike visited his old friends in Paterson.

He called on Katie Kane and her family, and received their congratulations.

"And now for the stage," he said, as he crossed to New York in the ferry-boat from Jersey City.

Mike had told his friends he had a surprise in store for them, and would sing a song appropriate to the occasion.

The night of his first appearance came.

He was very nervous.

"I wonder how I'll be received?" he asked Doc MacDonough, who was in charge of the front of the house.

"To-night will show how popular you are, Mike."

"Do you think any one will try to queer me?"

"Not in this house."

Mike was thinking of Billy Blake and his foolish threat of some time before.

He had not seen or heard of Billy, and he thought his silence was significant.

Before going on, Mike looked through a hole in the curtain.

He saw the boxes were filled with his friends, and this gave him courage.

"All ready, Mr. Kelly, your turn next," said the callboy.

Pulling himself together, Mike walked toward the wings.

"I must do or die," he muttered.

By this time he was in the glare of the foot-lights.

They blinded him.

The noise on his entrance was deafening.

"Speech, speech, speech," came from all parts of the house.

"Yes, let King Kelly give us a speech," cried Doc MacDonough.

Mike held up his hand for silence.

"I thank you, gentlemen," he said. "I didn't come here to make a speech. I came to sing. Let her go, Mr. Orchestra Leader."

As Mike ceased, the orchestra played the well-known air: "Casey at the Bat."

This song had been especially written for Mike.

The words were very funny, and told of the experiences of an Irishman on the ball field.

When he had sung three or four other songs Mike went off.

He was succeeded by a singer, who sang: "Slide, Kelly, slide."

This increased the enthusiasm.

It was a great night for Mike Kelly.

"Didn't I tell you you would become a great man, Mike," said Eddie Carter, when the two were alone that night.

"Yes; the people are very kind to me," said the famous pitcher.

Mike was thinking of the old days when he played ball with the Paterson Club.

"Yes, Eddie, I have done pretty well."

And every one else thought Mike had done pretty well.

He was one of the most popular men in the base-ball ranks.

The End

Appendix C: "Slide, Kelly, Slide!" Sheet Music and Lyrics

Written and Composed by J. W. Kelly. Copyrighted 1889, by Harding Bros., New York

I played a game of base ball, I belong to Casey's Nine!
The crowd was feeling jolly, and the weather it was fine;
A nobler lot of players I think were never found.
When the omnibuses landed that day upon the ground,
The game was quickly started, they sent me to the bat;
I made two strikes, says Casey, "what are you striking at?"
I made the third, the catcher muffed, and to the ground it fell;
I run like a devil to first base, when the gang began to yell:

CHORUS
Slide, Kelly, slide! Your running's a disgrace!
Slide, Kelly, slide! Stay there, hold your base!
If some one doesn't steal you, and your batting doesn't fail you,
They'll take you to Australia! Slide, Kelly, slide!

'Twas in the second inning they called me in, I think,
To take the catcher's place, while he went to take a drink;
But something was the matter, sure I couldn't see the ball;
And the second one that came in, broke my muzzle, nose and all.

The crowd up in the grand stand they yelled with all their might,
I ran toward the club house, I thought there was a fight.
'Twas the most unpleasant feeling I ever felt before;
I knew they had me rattled, when the gang began to roar:
Slide, Kelly, slide, &c.

They sent me out to centre-field. I didn't want to go,
The way my nose was swelling up, I must have been a show;
They said on me depended victory or defeat.
If a blind man was to look at us he's know that we were beat.
"Sixty-four to nothing!" was the score when we got done,
And ev'rybody there but me said they had lots of fun.
The news got home ahead of me, they heard I was knocked out,
The neighbors carried me in the house, and then began to shout:
Slide, Kelly, slide, &c.

2
SLIDE, KELLY, SLIDE!
COMIC SONG
Written & Composed by J.W. Kelly, for
MISS MAGGIE CLINE.
Moderato.
Fine.
1. I play'd a game of base-ball, I be-long to Ca-sey's Nine! The
2. 'Twas in the sec-ond in-ning They call'd me in, I think, To
3. They sent me out to cen-tre-field, I did-n't want to go; The
crowd was feel-ing jol-ly, And the wea-ther it was fine; A
take the catch-er's place, while He went to get a drink; But
way my nose was swell-ing up, I must have been a show! They
Copyright by F. Harding.

3
no - bler lot of players, I think were nev - er found. When the
something was the mat - ter, Sure I could - n't see the ball; And the
said on me de - pended Vic - t'ry or de - feat. If a
om - ni - bus - es land - ed That day up - on the ground, The
sec - ond one that came in, Broke my muz - zle, nose and all. The
blind man was to look at us, He'd know that we were beat.
game was quick - ly start - ed, They sent me to the bat: I
crowd up in the Grand Stand, They yelled with all their might; I
"Six - ty four to noth - ing!" Was the score when we got done, And

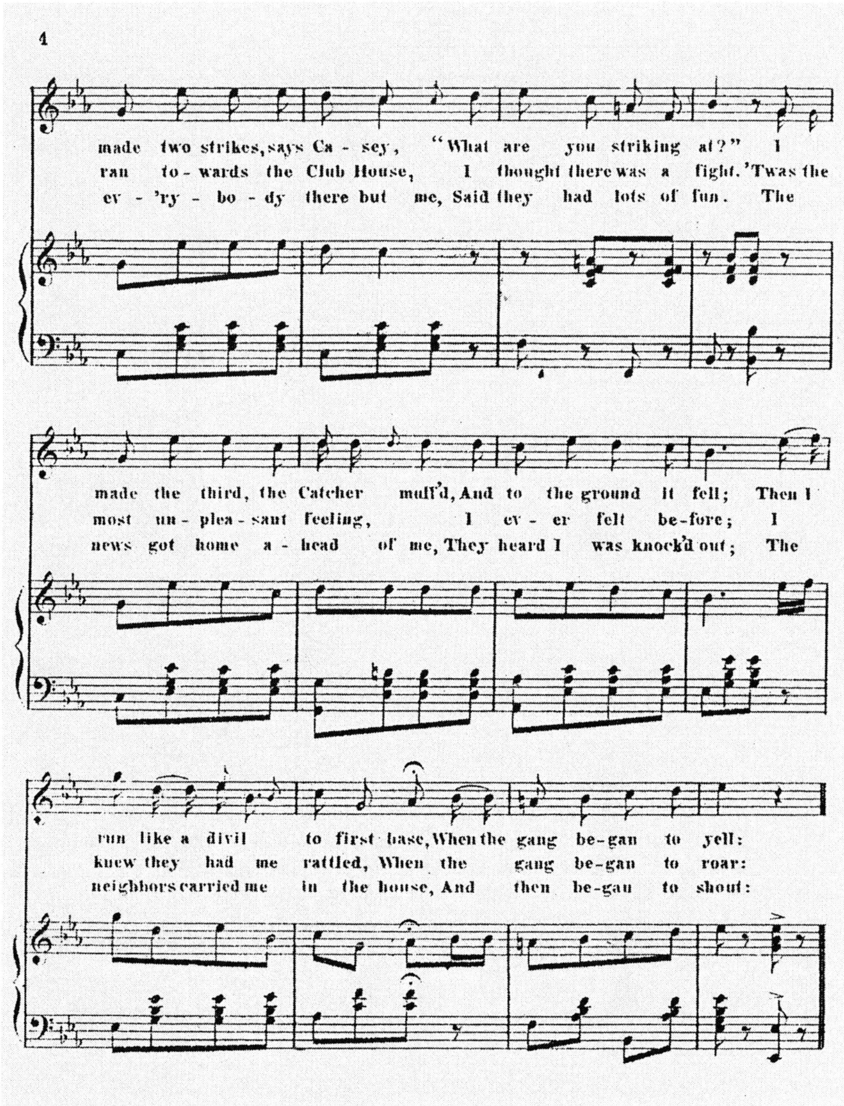
4
made two strikes, says Ca - sey, "What are you striking at?" I
ran to - wards the Club House, I thought there was a fight. 'Twas the
ev - 'ry - bo - dy there but me, Said they had lots of fun. The
made the third, the Catcher muff'd, And to the ground it fell; Then I
most un - plea - sant feeling, I ev - er felt be - fore; I
news got home a - head of me, They heard I was knock'd out; The
run like a divil to first base, When the gang be - gan to yell:
knew they had me rattled, When the gang be - gan to roar:
neighbors carried me in the house, And then be - gan to shout:

4
made two strikes, says Ca - sey, "What are you striking at?" I
ran to - wards the Club House, I thought there was a fight. 'Twas the
ev - 'ry - bo - dy there but me, Said they had lots of fun. The
made the third, the Catcher muff'd, And to the ground it fell; Then I
most un - plea - sant feeling, I ev - er felt be - fore; I
news got home a - head of me, They heard I was knock'd out; The
run like a divil to first base, When the gang be - gan to yell:
knew they had me rattled, When the gang be - gan to roar:
neighbors carried me in the house, And then be - gan to shout:

CHORUS.
5
Slide, Kel - ly, slide! Your runnings a dis - grace!
Slide, Kel - ly, slide! Stay there, hold your base! If
some one does - n't steal you, And your bat - ting does - n't fail you, They'll
take you to Aus - tra - lia! Slide, Kel - ly, slide!
D.S.

Appendix D: The One and Only Kell: Articles, Anecdotes, and Game Accounts, 1885–1938

The Sporting Life. May 27, 1885

Games Played May 18

PHILADELPHIA VS. CHICAGO AT PHILADELPHIA MAY 18—The home club outbatted and outfielded the visitors, but lost the game through poor base running, their excellence in this respect winning for the Western lads. The game was stubbornly contested on both sides from first to last. The visitors went in with the evident determination to win by hook or by crook, and they won by crook. Daly's pitching proved hard to hit, but Anson and his men were equal to the emergency. They played the game for all it was worth, resorting to numerous tricks intended to defraud and "rattle" the home club, and which secured them the ill will of the crowd. In one inning Kelly held Myers on second base and stopped him from making a double play, and at another time Williamson threw his arms around Fogarty and held him on third base, keeping him from scoring a run. The old trick of cutting across the diamond from short field home was tried. The Chicagos took exceptions to every ruling made by the umpire, and Mr. Cushman was rattled in more than one inning. Fogarty lost a run in the seventh inning by being caught off second base by a throw from Flint, and Daly was caught napping at first base by Clarkson in the eighth inning. Score:

CHICAGO	*T*	*R*	*B*	*P*	*A*	*E*	*PHILA*	*T*	*R*	*B*	*P*	*A*	*E*
Dalry'ple, lf	5	0	0	3	0	1	Manning, rf	5	1	3	1	0	0
Gore, cf	5	0	1	3	0	0	Andrews, lf	5	1	2	0	0	0
Kelly, rf	4	2	1	1	1	1	Myers, 2b	5	1	1	0	4	0
Anson, 1b	3	1	1	12	0	1	Lynch, cf	5	0	1	2	0	0
Pfeffer, 2b	4	1	0	2	1	1	Fogarty, ss	3	1	1	2	5	0
Will'ms'n, 3b	4	1	1	2	1	0	Mulvey, 3b	3	0	1	1	0	0
Burns, ss	4	1	1	0	3	0	Farrar, 1b	4	0	0	12	0	1
Clarkson, p	4	1	2	0	6	4	Daly, p	4	1	0	0	3	5
Flint, c	4	0	0	4	3	5	Clements, c	4	1	2	8	1	2
Total	37	7	7	27	15	13	Total	36	6	11	*26	13	8

*One out for interfering with fielder.

Chicago	0	3	1	0	0	0	1	2	0—7
Philadelphia	3	0	0	2	1	0	0	0	0—6

Runs earned—Chicago 3. Two-base hits—Anson, Williamson, Burns, Clarkson, Manning, Andrews and Myers. First on errors—Chicago 3, Philadelphia 2. First on balls—Kelly, Anson, Fogarty and Mulvey. Left on bases—Chicago 5, Philadelphia 7. Struck out—Dalrymple, Gore, Pfeffer and Lynch. Wild pitch—Daly. Passed balls—Flint 2, Clements 2. Time 2:05. Umpire—Cushman.

PROVIDENCE VS. CHICAGO AT PROVIDENCE MAY 21.—The first meeting of the season between these famous clubs was not a pleasant one for the champions, who were badly beaten, not scoring a run, while the Whites piled up ten. This disastrous defeat was the inability of the Grays to bat Clarkson. The Providence team played about as poor a game as can be imagined, while the visitors played well from the start. The umpiring was vile, but worse for the visitors than for the home team. The attendance was1,500. Kelly tried his old trick of knocking a ball out of Farrell's hand on Anson's hit, and both were declared out. Score:

PROV.	*T*	*R*	*B*	*P*	*A*	*E*	*CHICAGO*	*T*	*R*	*B*	*P*	*A*	*E*
Carroll, lf	4	0	2	4	0	1	Sunday, lf	3	1	2	2	0	0
Farrell, 2b	4	0	1	3	1	1	Gore, cf	3	1	2	1	0	0
Start, 1b	4	0	0	5	0	1	Kelly, rf	3	1	0	1	2	0
Irwin, ss	3	0	0	1	2	0	Anson, 1b	5	2	1	15	0	1
Hines, cf	3	0	0	1	0	0	Pfeffer, 2b	5	0	0	3	5	1

M'Corm'k, p	3	0	1	1	3	13	Wil'ms'n, 3b	4	3	1	2	2	0
Denny, 3b	3	0	0	1	2	1	Burns, ss	5	2	4	0	3	0
Gilligan, c	0	0	0	3	0	3	Clarkson, p	5	0	1	0	7	2
Dailey, c	1	0	1	3	1	1	Flint, c	4	0	0	3	0	0
Radford, rf	3	0	0	0	0	0							
Total	37	10	11	27	19	4	Total	28	0	5	*22	9	21

*Kelly and Anson out for interfering with fielder.

Chicago	0	1	4	0	1	0	2	2	x—10
Providence	0	0	0	0	0	0	0	0	0—0

Earned runs — Chicago 1. First on errors — Chicago 11, Providence 2. Struck out — Chicago 2, Providence 2. Left on bases — Chicago 9, Providence 5. Three-base hit — Clarkson. Two-base hits — Anson, Burns 2. Double plays — Chicago 3. Wild pitches — McCormick 6. Passed balls — Gilligan 1. Time —1:45. Umpire — Gaffney.

Boston Globe. October 12, 1886

Crack Fielders and Heavy Hitters

A Social Evening With Lieutenant Kelly, the Only Mike

His Witty Reminiscences and Points About the Game

McCormick's Verses and the $25 Chicago Fine

Big Ed Williamson, Fred Pfeffer, good natured and radiant, and Mike Kelly, the only, sat in the easiest chairs that the parlor of the Press Club affords and told stories. They had been helping Captain Anson win the League base ball championship and gave their exuberant spirits full play. "We play in Adams Tuesday and after that go to St. Louis to tackle the Browns, and you can wear balbriggan clothes all the winter by betting we'll win it easy. I think we'd 'a' batted hard today if there'd a' been a cannon there throwing the balls in. Yes, Rad did himself up the day before. I was walking out to the field after striking out, and I said to him: "I wish you would throw that arm of yours off of you. He never said a word. He's a terror. He fooled me dead on a couple of 'em. I thought they were up here across the neck just where I wanted 'em, but I couldn't 'a hit 'em with a ladder. I never strike at a low ball; I can't see 'em. Take my dying bath if I don't think I'm up to the top of the batting list after all — by the official averages, I mean, see? You cranks here don't know how to score ball. I ain't afraid of Anson, but Brouthers, he may be ahead of me. I ain't been watching what he's been doing these three or four days. I'm a little a-scared of him."

Then the great right-fielder, the great base-runner and the great catcher — Hanlon calls him the greatest — sat back in his seat and puffed violently at an Old Judge cigarette.

"Hanlon says he is afraid to try to steal bases on you, Mike," suggested the Champion Crank.

"A monkey can steal bases on me easy enough, but I'm always watching for a man like Hanlon. I'm right there close and they give me the balls a little wild so that I can throw 'em down. Ans and me can get down on most of 'em, though. He gives me time, or when I'm off I give him the fingers, you see? And he hits at a bad one or drops a little one where nobody can get it."

Kickers and Coaches

"John Morrill? He's the worst kicker in the business. Talk about Anson, he never kicks unless he has a right to gain his point."

"Or," interrupted Pfeffer, "unless we tell him to; then he'll make a bold bluff. So, Kel."

"Why, yes; but John, he keeps it up all the time. We don't kick. Take my dying bath if I ever say a word when Anson is talking, Eh, Old Whiskers?" turning to Williamson and winking slyly.

"Well," said the Champion Crank, "you are so good-natured about it, Mike, that the crowd likes it. They'd rather see you do it than not, but some of these fresh roosters, like Palsey Cahill, they make anybody weary. There are different kinds of chin. Now, it would be better for John Morrill if he would talk a little louder; they'd think he was a better captain."

"Yes, bet your life," said the only Kel. "Why, now, Miller, the catcher of the Pittsburgs, he's a fresh one. The day we got beat there I was playing third base and Miller was out side of me, making a lot of cheap chin. I says: 'Mr. Galvin,' — Jimmy Galvin was umpiring the game — 'stop the game and call this man in; he'll get us rattled.'"

"We get beat by those cheap clubs sometimes," explained Fred Pfeffer. "It don't pay to take chances where nothing depends. In Rochester I sprained an ankle, and had to lay off for League games six days, see? Ginger ale, please."

Stagging, Pitching, Telegrams

"That was nothing, though, to the Lannon-Hearld fight the other night. Why, that was the best slugging I ever saw; oh, Fred? That Lannon is a clinker. Did you notice how he got there every time with his right duke? I think he had Hearld done in the first round. But none of them has any business with Sullivan. When you're talking fight John I. is tarred."

"You ought to pitch, Kelly, in one of those exhibition games. They'd like to see you in the box," suggested a would-be crank.

"Why, I pitched a game last year against the Buffalos. Old Brouth he made a home run the very first thing, and then Jack Rowe got in a three-bagger. I retired. His Whiskers here went in for the next inning, but they knocked him around just as bad. Then old Pfef tried it. They couldn't knock him out of the box, 'cause there was no one else to put in."

The laugh was on Pfeffer, but Feather-weight spoke up and said: "I remember all the same. Fred, when you pitched a great game against the Bostons, and Chicago won it."

"You know that piece you wrote about me the last of July?" asked Kelly. "Well I sent a paper to a cousin of mine with that in it. I never saw the girl, but I had a mash from that out. I'll send her a telegram tonight. I've got a lot more to send, too: one to my wife, one to Spalding, one to Nat Goodam, and one to my sister in California. Here," and he pulled some papers out of the pocket of his black Prince Albert, "I got it here just what I'm going to say — no I ain't either, they're all in my ball clothes."

The Row In Detroit

"How about that row you and Burns had in Detroit?" asked the Champion Crank. "Did we get that straight, Kel?"

"No, you got it all wrong. We had beat 'em two straight, see, and they were all dead sore. Williamson and Burns and me — his Whiskers over there gets me into all my trouble — were coming out of the grounds and about 200 kids follied us up to the cab. Burns got inside and I climbed on the box.

When one of the gang threw a brick through window and hit Tom in the neck, it made me mad, you know, and I put after the kid, but a big fellow with whiskers tackled me. Well, I sized him up and saw he was as big as I was, and I says to myself: 'I got my ball clothes on, and so help me Anson, if I don't do you.' I chased him around the crowd for a minute, and finally let go at him with my left duke. Burns had follied me out, and he gave him another in the neck and he staggered. Tom's wrist is lame from it now; he couldn't play ball for a cent yesterday and he didn't go on today. Then a fellow in the crowd yelled 'lynch 'em' and Tom and me piled into the cab and escaped."

Key Got There Just the Same

After a high official of the Press Club had executed the famous, ancient, "Base Ball Song," the only Mike stepped to the piano, deposited his 186 pounds of sinew and shape on the plush-covered stool and sang a ditty to the most familiar tune in "The Tin Soldier," playing his own accompaniment with his own big, bruised hands. One verse ran thus:

Chicago has a ball club,
The best in the land.
A detective brought news,
That seven drank bouze.
And Burns with a smoke in his hand.
Twenty five it was the damage,
The club house suffered the pain,
The directors had gall,
But when we played ball
We got there, just the same.
Sweet violets, only a pansy blossom,
When the robins nest again, rats!

Fred Pfeffer joined his voice in with Kelly's as he warbled, and the two sat down [illegible] and laughing, amid great applause. "McCormick wrote that himself," said Mike. "Good, ain't it?" Oh that was rank, fining us that time $25 apiece. Why, Spalding pulled us all up before him and read off all we had been doing, according to the detective, the son of a gun. He had Burns down smoking cigarettes and McCormick drinking three soda lemonades — Mac spoke up and said that wasn't true; one would kill him — and me having three bottles of beer in my room; and I says, 'What only three;

take my dying bath I never drank anything in my life, and his Old Whiskers over there doing everything that's wrong. He always gets me into trouble.

"Yes," broke in Pfeffer, "it was dead wrong. There we had been winning sixteen out of seventeen games, and when we started East afterwards we lost six out of ten, and that liked to have done us."

"Remember," said Kelly, "young Ryan owned up to drinking beer three times, and said it was because the water didn't agree with him? I see *one* of you fellows called him 'Fresh' in the papers the other day, wasn't it?"

All this time Williamson didn't say much, but only talked quietly at one side, and smiled at Kelly and admired him, and withal acted like the fat, good natured, homely, earnest fellow that he is. "After all," said Kelly, "they abuse us everywhere we go, but they like to see us play ball, all the same." When the party broke up the champions walked to their hotel, and the Champion Crank and the other cranks went home. The cold October sun peeked up State street and almost caught them all in the act.

Figuring the Averages

After a morning of solid sleep the Champion Crank and the other cranks woke in prime condition to figure out the League averages. The rendezvous was in a conveniently located garret on Beacon street. It was a big job, and it took a long time. Besides the accompanying tables, which represent six months of careful bookkeeping, many choice base ball thoughts were evolved. These are some of the expressions let drop:

Joe Hornung hasn't made but seven errors the whole season. He's kicking like a steer about that one we gave him the other day. It was an error, all the same. His average is .971; the highest last year was .941, Gillespie's. But old Gillesp doesn't go for balls that Joe does.

No; .296 isn't too large for Carroll.

These fellows that play all over the deck you have to be careful; Phil Baker, for instance.

I set out to bring in a bushel of pears for you, but I was too tired. Take a good rest tonight and bring them in tomorrow.

"Dupee" Shaw has a big average. How big? .094.

What a disappointment that man Crane was this year! Yes, the South Boston boy.

These Washington averages bother me. Well, it's hard to divide nothing by something.

Whew! Anson's percentage for singles is .371 and for totals .546.

I'm rattled; let's go to dinner.

Here's plenty of mucilage.

Too bad they didn't get there. They broke up at the last minute. The Fergie was too much for them.

What good honest ball the Phillies did play, too.

Here's old Carroll, left field all the time. He's a regular, he is, like Bill Carroll of South Boston.

You know the easiest club to figure? The Detroits, because they play in their postion.

Thanks; I haven't smoked a cigarette since I was in college.

Hardie Richardson's batting has been something wonderful lately.

My arm is getting very lame, but I'll try to pitch it through.

Mr. William Ewing. Thought his name was Buck.

John Ward, short stop all the time. He's taken mighty good care to play nowhere else.

We won't give Finley any fielding average. A wise decision. Getting razzle-dazzled?

Do you know how to figure the fielding? You don't, do you, Tom?

Think of Jim O'Rourke being .308. Low for Jeems.

How many are nine times eight? Seventy-two. Rats!

Here's old Burdie. He's played sixty games at second and I'll bet he's got a darned good average, too.

They'll buy this all in the morning for two cents, but they won't realize the amount of work there is in it.

How many wild pitches have you made tonight?

Richardson? Yes; 188 hits; more than any other man in the League.

Ganzell made a hit to a game.

Figure Brouthers right there. It will be close between him and Ans. and Kel.

Hanlon, 126 games, every one.

Old Bennett has beaten himself. Let's see. Last year he led with .885. This year it is .913.

Next year if I have anything to do with base ball, bet your life I'll keep this book up every day. Whiskers!

Jimmy Manning will lead the left fielders. No he won't either.

Here's Kel's batting—.868 for singles and .516 for totals. No, that don't beat Anson's.

I haven't got my watch with me. How much did you raise on it?

Here, give this to the gang. We are the gang.

This man Baker is a good one. What's his average? That's what I'm trying to find out.

Four—eleven. Forty-four.

I am simply to perform the long division, am I? It will be very long.

Well, I have my opinion of a man who can't read his own figures. He is hardly worth replying to, is he?

Give me some cube root, will you, before long? Won't a che-root do?

What are they going to put up there opposite S. S. Pierce's building? The public library. The public library? Yes. Too far down town. No; I mean Pierce's building on the Back Bay.

Jove! Is that right for Dorgan, less than .300?

These New Yorks are hard, too; it's dividing something by something. You fellows are hard to suit.

You been on Start ever since? Yes; can't somebody make a pun on the word?

What was Kelly drinking last night? Sarsaparilla.

New York Times. February 10, 1887

NO CHICAGO FOR KELLY.

But He Would Like To Toss Ball For The Giants.

Michael Kelly, the young man who has gained fame as a member of the Chicago Baseball Club and to whose efforts the success of the League champions can be attributed, was seen yesterday. He is in good condition and is hard at work getting ready for the opening of the season.

"Have you signed a contract with the Chicagos yet?" he was asked.

"No, Sir," was his response. "And, what is more, I don't intend to."

"Why, I was under the impression," said the reporter, "that Mr. Spalding and yourself had settled your difficulties and you were to rejoin his club."

"Mr. Spalding," he answered, "has led people to believe that I will again aid his club to win championship laurels, but, nevertheless, it is not so. I said at the close of last season that I would never again throw a ball as a member of the Chicago Club, and I repeat it now. I felt then that I had been shabbily treated, and I think so now, and for that reason I have not changed my mind. The baseball public regarded my threat as the mere assertion of a dissatisfied player, who would come to terms before the season opened. They are beginning to realize now that I mean what I said. Don't you think so?"

"Has there been any difference of views regarding the question of salary?"

"I was perfectly satisfied with the amount of salary that I received, but my objection to becoming a member of the Chicago Club for 1887 was solely because I would have to play under Spalding, Anson & Co. I would gladly accept an offer from the New-York Club for the same amount if I could procure an honorable release from Chicago. If Mr. Spalding refuses to let me go, I will retire on my laurels; but if he should decide to release me, I would be pleased to become a member of the New-York Giants. The managers of the Giants are good business men, and the New-York public appreciate good work, and for these reasons I would like to play here. The New-Yorks will make a strong bid for the championship honors during the coming season. They have been strengthened wonderfully by the engagement of George Gore, who is a ball player every inch of him. Keefe and Welch, I think, will be aided by the new rules, and if a good man can be secured to cover third base I think Mutrie's aggregation will have a first mortgage on the championship.

"In regard to the story published," he continued, "that I said that Ewing and Ward were the only ball players in the New-York Club, I will say that I never made use of that assertion. If it were so it would not be policy for me to say it. I have been playing too long to overlook such players a 'Jim' O'Rourke, 'Mike' Dorgan, 'Tim' Keefe, Rodger Connor, 'Joe' Gerhardt, and several other men who are on the Giants' pay roll, and I would be regarded as an imbecile if I claimed that they are not ball players."

New York Times. February 18, 1887

THE BASEBALL LEAGUE.

A Special Meeting Called — Kelly's Release By Chicago.

WASHINGTON, FEB. 17. — In accordance with suggestions from Messrs.

Day, of the New-York Baseball Club, and Spalding, of the Chicagos, President Young this afternoon issued a call for a meeting of the special committee of the League at Pittsburg next Monday to consider the question of the eighth club in the League for the ensuing season. "I have noticed the representatives of the Indianapolis, Kansas City, and St. Louis Clubs of this action," said Mr. Young, "and they will doubtless all be present. Whatever we do in the matter will be binding and must be unanimous. When we were appointed a committee we were given absolute power, and we could buy out the St. Louis or any other club and locate it at Kalamazoo if we saw fit. Ratification by the entire League is only a matter of form, and whatever we do will stand as the opinion of the entire body. All the negotiations thus far have been conducted by the Western clubs interested with Mr. Spalding, who is in reality the Chairman of the special committee, and he will submit everything bearing upon the question to us at the Monongahela House, in Pittsburg, next Monday. I have no doubt that we will be able to reach a satisfactory solution of the problem ere we adjourn. Of course the city that makes the best and most feasible proposition will be given representation as the eighth city in our circuit. There has been some doubt expressed whether or not the Boston Club actually paid $10,000 for Kelly," continued Mr. Young. "To settle misgivings on that point, here is a letter that I sent to Mr. Spalding last Tuesday:

Washington, Feb. 15, 1887
A. G. Spalding, Esq., President, &c.:

SIR: Inclosed herewith I hand you draft of National Bank of Redemption. Boston, Mass., on National Park Bank of New-York for ten thousand, ($10,000.) dated Feb. 12, 1887, in payment for release of M. J. Kelly. The draft is payable to order of J. B. Billings, Treasurer, and by him indorsed: "Pay the Chicago Ball Club or order. J. B. Billings. Treasurer." Please acknowledge receipt by wire immediately. Respectfully, N. E. YOUNG.

POUGHKEEPSIE, N. Y., FEB. 17.—Kelly, the ball player, said to-day that he didn't care to reply to Spalding's charge that he drank while with the Chicagos, but said he didn't drink to excess. He said he took a drink now and then, and will take a glass of beer whenever he wants one. He spoke well of the Chicago Club and people there, but complained that he was not promoted as expected. He said he was promised the Captaincy of the Chicago Club for three years, and got tired waiting. Even if he hadn't signed with the Boston people, he would not have gone back to Chicago. He said the

Chicago managers got $10,000 for letting him go, and that it was like picking the money up on the street, for they knew he would not go back. He was making $3,200 a year with the Chicagos, whereas with the Boston people he will make $5,000 or more. He says he and his wife will sail for Europe next Saturday and return about the 20th of March, so as to be able to commence playing with the Bostons by the 1st of April. He goes to Europe to get rid of letters and talk.

Brooklyn Eagle. February 20, 1887

SPORT-PASTIME DRIFT.

Magnificent Salaries for Professional Players.

The National Game One of the Most Profitable Industries of the Country—$15,000 for a Catcher—The Boston's Gain and the Chicago's Loss—Minor Base Ball Matters—Chess and Cricket.

The important question of the day in professional managerial base ball circles is, "What are base ball players' salaries coming to?" A dozen years ago $1,000 for a first class player's services for the season of six months' field service was regarded as the fancy price of the period, the majority of the salaries then ranging form $500 to $900 a season. What is the fancy price of the present period? According to the latest deal in procuring a player's services in the professional market for 1887 the fancy figures reach $15,000! for that is the price the Boston Club will pay this year for the services of *Mike Kelly* of the Chicago team, as captain and catcher of the Boston team. First they pay $10,000—by certified check—to the Chicago Club for his release. Then they pay him $2,000—contract price—for his services as a player, and $3,000 for his additional services as the captain of the team. The deal was the sensation of the past week in the base ball centers of the country, and all sorts of opinions have been ventilated in regard to the action taken by the Boston Club in the matter. Of course, the prominent queries were "Will it pay the Bostons to give such a sum for a player?" and "Can the Chicago Club afford to let Kelly go?" Looking at the purchase of Kelly's release in the light of the speculative investment, I think it will pay the Boston Club well. In the first place, their club needs a local booming, and

Kelly's presence in the team will undoubtedly give it. Then the team requires a captain who can thoroughly rule the players and inspire them with new confidence in their ability to win, as Harry Wright used to do in the old Boston team; and this Kelly will bring about. As to whether Chicago can afford to let *Kelly* go, all there is to be said about that, is, the fact that they have $10,000 in hand in the way of good reason for their action, not to mention the fact that *Kelly* had become a dissatisfied member of the team and did not want to play any more in Chicago. With Kelly's release the Chicago Club loses the services of the last and best of their three veteran out-fielders; but in their places their treasury is enriched by $14,000 and that, too, before a single game of 1887 has been played. They now have three good outfielders in Ryan, Sunday, and Flynn, and to take the places of Dalrymple, Gore and Kelly, and the new men are all ambitious of rivaling the prestige of the absentees, and who will play the positions at about half the cost the veterans could have been retained for. But it will be difficult to replace Kelly's services as a base runner and skillful strategist on the field. There are, however, the cash reasons for letting the trio go, and moreover, the new policy of the club in insisting upon strictly temperate habits in their players which is opposed to the retention of drinking men in the newly organized team. There is, however, an underlying question involved in this very costly deal made by the Boston Club, and that is, "What will be its effect on the salary question of the future?" Ten thousand dollars for a release, with the addition of $5,000 salary pales all the previous fancy figures of the base ball market. The question now is whether such comparatively moderate salaries as $2,500 or $3,000 a season won't be regarded as past figures for coming professional celebrities? It would seem as if $5,000 would now be the coming figures for regular salaries. It may be just possible that this *Kelly* deal, with its $15,000 cost, will be the culminating point of the salary question, and hereafter a decline in prices will follow. The circumstances connected with the latest deal are very exceptional. Not another club in the country is so situated as to afford to pay half the price for Kelly's services that the Boston Club has done. A noteworthy effect of this last and greatest of the Winter base ball sensations is the effect it has had on transfering the interest in deals from the West to the East. The Boston Club is now the central figure in the base ball picture, and a great boom will set in there from this time out. It is somewhat singular that two surprises would have been sprung upon the base ball world the same day, viz: the *Kelly* deal and the secession of the Harvard, Yale and Princeton clubs from the Intercollegiate Association, followed by the establishment of a special college league, embracing only the clubs of these three noted universities. That this move of the three colleges is a good one there is no doubt. In the first place, it will center the interest of the college championship in the three clubs which have hitherto taken the lead each season in the college arena; and, secondly, it will oblige the Intercollegiate Association to extend its sphere of operations so as to embrace every college club of note of the Middle and Eastern States outside of the three seceding colleges. Now that Harvard, Yale and Princeton are out of the way there will be an excellent opening for a very even contest for championship honors among the clubs of Bowdoin, Dartmouth, Amherst, Williams, Brown and Trinity in the East, and Cornell, Columbia, Stevens, Rutgers, Pennsylvania University and Lafayette of the Middle States section. Verily, matters are exciting and sensational in the base ball world at present.

NOTES OF THE WEEK.

The New York Club's reserve corps, now under charge of Manager Becannon, includes his brother James as pitcher, with Charles Gaunt and Jerry Totten as catchers and Richard Cooke, A. K. Hutchins and W. J. Roberts as base players.

John Daily, of this city, is likely to be appointed as one of the International League umpires. He is a good man for the position.

The new American Association umpires for 1887 are John McQuade, E. Cuthbert, A. Knight and A. Bauer.

The *Boston Herald* says that Burdock has no just right to complain of harsh treatment at the hands of the Boston Club simply because it will not release him at the call of any club. Mr. Stevens says:

> He is indebted to the club for nearly $1,000 for money advanced to the support of his family when he was not in a position to return an equivalent by playing ball, and if the directors are endeavoring to secure a reimbursement of the same they can hardly be blamed. I was the first to recommend Burdock to Harry Wright a dozen years ago, as a very promising player and as an honest player, the latter an important matter in the crooked ways of that period. I regret to note his fall from grace as regards habits of temperance and his consequent loss of position in the ranks, and I trust to see him reform and recover his lost prestige.

Mr. Brand writes as follows in relation to the Vernon Club:

In your Sunday's issue you publish Seabury & Johnson as being managers of the Vernon Base Ball Club. This is incorrect. Be kind enough to mention in your next Sunday's base ball items that all communications relating to games, time of playing, etc., should, to insure attention, be addressed to me below.

JOHN BRAND,
452 Lafayette avenue.

The Baltimore Club has been scheduled to play exhibition games from March 30 to April 15, as follows: They open with the Pennsylvania University and then play in regular order the Philadelphia team, Amherst College, the Buffalos, Williams College, the Boston team — three days — Yale College and the Syracuse Stars. They then begin the championship games on the 15th.

The Brooklyn exhibition season will open in April with two games with Manager Hackett's Newark team, the first in Brooklyn and the return in Newark.

The Detroit Club is to open in Charleston, playing there four days, beginning March 30.

All the American Association Club players are to report at their respective headquarters by March 15 — not a month distant.

That earnest, steady, reliable player, Jimmy Clinton, has been wisely engaged by the Nashville Club. Catcher Jack Hayes, who is a fine player when in proper form, will also catch for the same club.

The Boston team for 1887 now bids fair to be as follows: *Kelly*, captain and catcher; Radbourne, pitcher; Morill (manager), Higgins and Nash on the bases; Glasscock, short stop, and Hornung, Johnston and Peerman in the outfield, with Stemmyer and Daily and Conway and Gunning as extra batteries, and Higgins, Wise, O'Rourke and Madden as substitutes. Pitcher Bufinton, Third Baseman Sutton, Second Baseman Burdock and Catchers Tate and Murphy are open for release to any club wishing them for a bonus.

The *Sporting Life* says:

President Stern, of the Cincinnati Club, received a personal letter from John B. Day recently, in which he stated positively that the New York Club was in need of McCormick's services, and that if Spalding released him he would be at once signed by the New York Club.

I don't think Spalding is going to let McCormick go unless "Al" finds it impossible to hold him to temperate habits, in which case New York can have him.

The St. Louis champions — Chris. Von der Abe's

Boston Globe. March 29, 1887

THE LATEST KELLY STORY.

Jim Mutrie's Tale of the Aptness of Genial Mike.

"Handsome Jeems" gives the latest tale about Mike Kelly as follows:

"I must tell you a little story about Kelly. I have seen a good many clever things done on the ball field, but a little performance of Kelly's on the Polo grounds last summer lays over them all. The game was almost finished, and was two to nothing in our favor. Kelly was on second, when Anson pounded one of those corkers he hits to right field. 'Kel' made a dash for home. I don't know whether he touched third or way between home and third. It happened that the gate under the grand stand was open and the ball rolled through. Mike had his eye on it, and when he had crossed the plate and scored he never stopped running, but made straight for that passage-way. Tom Deasley and Tim Keefe had both made a break for the ball, and were under the grand stand hustling for it. Quick as a dash Kelly shut the gate and stood in front of it, holding his hands over his head and flourishing them about wildly, so that he completely prevented our boys from getting out with the ball or throwing it over his head. All this time Kelly was yelling, 'Go it, Ans, go it, Ans,' and Ans did go it. He didn't stop until he had gone clear round the bases and had scored a run.

"All the other Chicago players saw the ball go through that gate, but not one of them was quick-witted enough to take the chance which Kelly saw in a second. I can tell you there are a plaguey few Kellys."

Boston Daily Globe. May 10, 1887

TESTIMONIAL TO M.J. KELLY.

The Great Player Feasted and Presented With a Beautiful Token of Regard.

Last fall a party of eight gentlemen, all members of Boston Lodge of Elks, visited Chicago. While there they were royally entertained by the members of the Chicago ball club, and particularly by Michael J. Kelly. They had such a good time that they voted then and there that when Kelly came to Boston this season they would get up some testimonial of their regard and present it to Kelly on the ball field. At that time none of the gentlemen imagined that Kelly would be a member of the Boston team. As soon as it was decided that the great player would certainly come to the Hub, the gentlemen in question, Messrs. John Graham, Lewis D. Jones, E. C. Donnely, J. Lewis White, Lewis Lyford, R. L. Frampton and John F. Courtney, immediately proceeded to put their scheme in progress. They spoke of it to others, and soon discovered that many who were friends of the "only Kel" were anxious to join in the testimonial to him. The pressure was too great to withstand, and the originators of the scheme were obliged to change their plans. It was finally decided to tender Kelly a banquet under cover of which the presentation should be made. The carefully-planned affair came off last night at the Hall on Hayward place.

The occasion was one long to be remembered. Over fifty gentlemen were gathered about the well-filled banquet tables. Fred E. Atteaux presided. On his right was His Honor Mayor Hugh O'Brien; next to him came Michael J. Kelly, and on Mr. Kelly's right sat Charles Reed and John Graham. To the left of Mr. Atteaux sat Colonel Boyd, interpreter to Queen Kapiolani, and John F. Dever. Among other gentlemen present were Alderman William P. Carroll, Frazier Coulter, Edward B. Daily, Dr. A. B. Heath, Christopher Connor, J. C. Morse, John T. Fynes, John J. Droban, W. I. Harris, Justin S. Keeler, Charles Thorn, Joseph L. White, George W. Floyd, Charles W. Perkins, George Schiller and others.

When the elaborate spread had been thoroughly examined, tested and found perfect, Mr. Atteaux arose and, in a few well-chosen word, explained how the company had been brought together, and said that to show how deeply the Elks who had been entertained at Chicago appreciated the courtesies extended on that occasion had with the aid of others of his friends prepared a little surprise for Mr. Kelly, and that Mayor O'Brien had kindly consented to make the presentation.

Mayor O'Brien arose and was greeted with much applause. He said:

> Mr. President and Gentlemen of the Elks — I assure you it is a great relief to throw off all official restraints and appear among you tonight, because when I look around this table I know you are all jolly good fellows. (Applause and laughter.)
>
> Now I have no doubt that Mr. Kelly, said His Honor the Mayor, is very much surprised tonight. I had occasion to go to Brooklyn a few evenings ago, and they urged me

to talk about municipal affairs. In so doing I made the remark that Boston had the most expensive city government in the country, because we want the best of everything. Now, I don't believe that any other city in the country has so good a lodge of Elks as we have in Boston. (Applause.) I know a great deal of their charitable work and the good they are accomplishing.

The national game is always a very attractive game in Boston, and we want the best ball player in the country, and I believe we've got him. (Great applause.) Now, Mr. Kelly, allow me to present you on behalf of your friends this token of their kind regard and remembrance. (Applause.)

His honor then handed Mr. Kelly a black case containing a watch chain and locket. The orchestra in attendance played "For he's a jolly good fellow," and the gentlemen present joined in the refrain.

Kelly took the case in his hand, and when the applause had subsided said: "Mr. Mayor and gentlemen — This is quiet a surprise for me and I have had a good many. I had one in Philadelphia lately, and again today, but I hope we will get even with them tomorrow.

I have found my stay in Boston a very pleasant one so far, and I'm afraid if I stay much longer you'll ruin me with kindness. If I had my ball clothes on and was a good ways off I could talk to you, but I've got stage fright on me now so I can only thank you very much for this beautiful gift, and assuring you that I will never part with it, remain yours truly, Osmond Tearle." (Great applause and laughter.) Someone called out, "What's the matter with M. J. Kiley," and the response "He's all right" almost shook the house. Mr. Kelly was followed in brief speeches and recitations by Alderman Carroll, Frazier Coulter, George Thorne, J. L. White, Charlie Reed and others, the festivities being continued until a late hour.

The testimonial to Mr. Kelly consists of an elegant Howard gold watch, a heavy gold chain of long links weighing 56 penny-weights, and a square gold locket. The front of the watch has an engraved likeness of Kelly in his base ball suit, and the reverse of the case is ornamented with an elk's head. Inside is the inscription: "Presented to M. J. Kelly by Members of Boston Lodge of Elks and Other Friends at Boston, May 9, 1887."

The locket is a work of art. On the front is Kelly's monogram, the letter "K." being set in diamonds. On the reverse is an elk's head. The eyes are made of rubies, and beneath is a handsome diamond. Inside is a picture of Kelly's wife. The charm on the chain is a miniature bat of gold, made in the shape of a pencil, with an onyx ball on the end of it. The subscribers to the testimonial were:

Nathaniel Goodwin, Jr.,
George W. Floyd,
E. S. Innes,
M. Mullane,
Frank W. Sawyer,
H. Emerson,
James Backley,
F. E. Atteaux,
Dr. A. B. Heath,
G. H. Hastings,
John Graham,
Charlie Reed,
Charles W. Perkins,
W. J. Anderson,
A. L. Thompson,
L. H. Lyford,
James A. Blake,
J. Louis White,
Daniel Hurley,
Joseph L. White,
Lewis L. Jones,
M. L. Alley,
W. H. Petters,
Samuel Well,
J. S. Keeler,
Fred B. Anderson,
George Wood,
F. B. Anderson,
W. A. Miller,
Charles H. Hoyt,
Frank H. Mudge,
Thomas A. Daly,
James W. Treadwell,
Fred Alford,
E. D. Chase,
John F. Canahan,
Frazier Coulter,
G. H. Jones,
E. B. Daily,
G. E. Hayden,
John H. Dee,
John F. Dever,
S. Bacharach,
Nathaniel M. Merrick,
William Daly, Jr.,
L. Kennedy,
Frank J. McCarthy,
J. J. Murphy,
William Harris,
C. J. Connelly,
James T. Powers,
George Thorne,
J. O. Gray,
Phillip Branson,
Charles W. Quinn,
D. A. Dunbar, Jr.,
James McLane,
C. F. Kendall,
B. S. Flanders,
A. H. Dean,
H. A. Buck,
D. B. Newell,
J. L. White,
C. A. Buckley,
C. A. Jones,
W. P. Carroll,
Joseph Robinson,
E. C. Donnelly,
P. A. Sheehan,
A. C. Simmons,
John C. Manning,
W. W. Tillotson,
Dr. Eaton,
T. J. Fuller,
C. E. Rice,
G. A. Schiller,
H. J. Seller,
Mark Price,
I. H. Dinner,
A. W. Savin.

Each gentleman present was given a beautiful souvenir of the occasion, containing a splendid portrait of Kelly.

Boston Globe. October 9, 1887

CAPTAIN MIKE KELLY

Winner of The Globe's Gold Medal for Base Running.

Michael Joseph Kelly, captain of the Bostons, winner of The Globe's gold medal for champion base runner of his team and the acknowledged king of the base ball profession, was born at Troy, N. Y., Dec. 31, 1857. His family moved to Washington, D. C., when Kelly was quiet young, and he began playing ball with the Keystone Juniors. In 1873 the family went to Paterson, N. J., and Kelly joined the Haymakers, with whom he remained two years as right fielder. His first professional engagement was with the Olympics of

Paterson, 1876–7, and in 1878 he went to Columbus, O., where he played with the Buckeyes. In 1879 he joined the Cincinnati league club as catcher. In 1880 Kelly was captured by the Chicago club, with whom he has remained ever since.

It has been said that a man's record rarely shows his ability as a player. This is to a limited extent true, certainly it is so in Kelly's case. No figures could possibly give, to a man who has never seen him on the field, any idea of his wonderful and almost ceaseless activity on the diamond, the phenomenal work he does, and the influence he exerts upon the members of his own team.

In 1879 Kelly ranked fourth among league batsmen, with an average of .348. In 1882 he ranked eighth among batsmen with .305, and sixth as a fielder with .887. In 1885 he stood fifteenth as a batter with .287, and twenty-first as a fielder with .868; as a catcher, he was sixteenth on the list with .760. Last season he played 116 games, and according to The Globe's figures ranked second as a batter, with a single average of .368 and a total base average of .516. Nick Young, in his official figures, gives him something over .870 and the first place. He stood tenth among the catchers with .889, and seventeenth among right-fielders with .717. As an all-round player he ranked No. 24 with .800.

The above figures seem inconsistent with the title generally bestowed upon him as the prince of players, yet nevertheless the title is well merited. His abilities as a coacher and base runner are remarkable. He has a record of 15 seconds in covering the bases. He has earned the reputation of being the most daring base runner and the cleverest "kicker" of a "kicking team," and yet the more he kicks the more the crowds delight in him. He is better known and sooner recognized than any man on the diamond. Everybody knows him because everybody watches him. His fielding and batting are always good; but if it were possible to strike an average of steadiness at the bat, conscientious fielding, persistent kicking, skilful base getting and a knowledge of all the tricks that help to win, he would easily stand without a peer.

Mike is frequently called "the only Kell," and aptly, too, because he does things that no other player ever does, or can do, unless he could assume Mike's nature, without bringing himself into the disfavor of the public. One of Kelly's most memorable feats was to score once on a time from second base without going near third, a very hard thing to do in the league and get away with it.

Personally Kelly is not a handsome man, and yet no one would call him homely. He is 5 feet 10 inches in height, and weighs about 170 pounds. His face is swarthy and sunburned, and his hair and moustache black. He is undoubtedly, with the possible exception of Jimmy Galvin, the best-natured man who plays ball for money, rarely losing his temper, and seldom, if ever, making an exhibition of it. He possesses a peculiar faculty of sizing up a crowd, and seems to know instinctively just how much they will stand. In victory he is jubilancy itself, but defeat, no matter how severe, cannot crush him, although several times during the present season continued reverses have somewhat affected his ordinarily good temper. As a rule, however, he takes things as they come, the good and the bad, without openly flinching.

Kelly's base running this year has been of the best. Not only has he won The Globe medal, but he has outstripped every base-runner in the league, save Ward and Fogarty, in the number of bases stolen, and considering his chances, has more than equalled the performances of either player. Take him all and all, Kelly is, beyond a doubt, the best base-runner in the National League.

Brooklyn Eagle. April 17, 1889

Earned runs — Brooklyn, 3; Philadelphia, 12. First base by errors — Brooklyn, 4; Philadelphia, 4; Battery errors — Brooklyn, 7; Philadelphia, 11. Left on bases — Brooklyn, 10; Philadelphia, 6. Stolen bases — Brooklyn, 6; Philadelphia, 2. Total bases — Brooklyn, 12; Philadelphia, 32. Struck out — Brooklyn, 3; Philadelphia, 3. Chances for catches — Brooklyn, 9; Philadelphia, 3. Double plays — Brooklyn, 2. Bases on balls — By Terry, 3; by Gleason, 6. Wild pitches — By Terry, 4: by Gleason, 1. Hit batsman — By Gleason, 1. Passed balls — Decker, 3. Umpire — Ferguson. Time — 2 hours and 10 minutes.

The Boston reporters whom Mike Kelly called "ham fatters" are getting square on the $10,000 player. Mr. Morse, of the *Boston Herald*, who is with the Boston team on their tour to Baltimore, while in Philadelphia last week had a talk with Mr. Spalding about Kelly, and it so interesting that it is given below for the Eagle readers to dwell upon. Mr. Morse asked Mr. Spalding if he expected Kelly to go on the trip, and he replied:

"To answer that question properly I will have to include a matter that is not exactly included in it, yet touches it. All the members of our party who wanted to go made requests to go; we asked no one. Before our party was made up we asked Mr. Comiskey, of the St. Louis Club, and Mr. McPhee, of the Cincinnati, to accompany us out of compliment to the American Association. The former was unable to go on account of pressing business that demanded his attention, the latter on account of an injury to his leg. Mr. Kelly made application with others. Before he signed I told him that I could not pay him very much money, and he said that was all right. He wanted to go. He signed his contract. He failed to keep it, as is well known. Every effort was made to have him go on the trip. I had a talk with him in Chicago before we left for the coast, and urged him to go as far as the coast, for we had billed him. He finally said that he would go East, fix up things and join us. I gave him $100 for expenses. We looked for him at Denver, and expected him daily. He stayed away, and so did my $100. I never invited him to join the party abroad, in London or Paris, and I most positively deny that I ever abrogated the contract he made with me to go on the trip. I am heartily glad that he did not go. Oceans of wine were set before us, and to a man of Kelly's appetite such an attraction would have been too inviting, and I am sure he would not have been able to resist. I am sorry that the Boston Club has such a man as its captain. He does not rank with those the club has had in the past. I feel almost ashamed that I sold such bad goods to the Boston Club. He isn't the Kel that he used to be when in the Chicago Club." Here Anson chimed in: "That is straight, all of it. I hear that Kel has said that it was no wonder that Chicago could not win because I could not catch a little bit, not even a railroad. Well, I don't pose as a catcher, but from what I saw of Kelly on Thursday he would have hard work to catch a horse car. What have they been thinking of, to let John Morrill go — a man who stood as high as any other man in the profession?"

The experience of allowing league players to keep saloons like that *Mike Kelly* has in charge has led Mr. Spalding to take action at the league meeting this year to prevent players or others connected with the league from being associated in any way with the proprietorship or running of liquor places. Kelly's day is about over. The saloon influence has ruined him.

New York Times. November 25, 1889

A NEW BROTHERHOOD MAN

"KING" KELLY JOINS THE BALL PLAYERS' LEAGUE.

He Is Engaged To Play In Boston At A Salary Of $5,000 Per Annum.

Michael J. Kelly, the Captain of the Boston Baseball Club, better known, perhaps, as the "Ten-Thousand-Dollar Beauty," or the "King of the Diamond," attached his signature to a Brotherhood contract this morning shortly after midnight. This is considered a victory for the Brotherhood. Kelly is, perhaps, one of the most prominent players on the diamond. He has a following second to none, and it is supposed that many who at present are on the fence will shortly follow his example.

Kelly has been in sympathy with the new movement from the outset, but he did not take an active part in the formation of the clubs for private reasons. He assured the boys that he was with them, heart and soul, and that when called upon to render assistance he would respond at once. When asked to sign a contract he said that he would prefer to wait until the Spring. Emissaries of the old Boston Club have been in town of late making flattering offers to him, and, while the Brotherhood people placed the greatest confidence in Kelly's word, they thought that it would be more suitable to have him attach his name to a contract. When Glasscock, Denny, McKean, and other shining lights left the Brotherhood the backers began to grow a tride fearful. In order to assure them that the stars were in favor of the movement, Ward, who was in the West, sent Al Johnston of Cleveland here to induce Kelly to sign a contract. Johnston arrived here yesterday, and when he stated the object of his mission Kelly asked for the contract, saying: "I want to show the boys that I am with them."

Without any ceremony he attached his signature to the document. Kelly will get a yearly salary of $5,000 for three years. He will also act in the capacity of manager. Kelly will go to work at once to get all the players of his club under contract. Clarkson, Ganzel, and Brouthers are the three who have not been put under contract; but he feels certain that he will bring them into the fold. "We have got a great club down there," he said, "and I'm going to prove that I know a thing or two about handling a team. My mission on earth from to-day is to help to make the new League a success. I will leave nothing undone to accomplish that object. If I am not mistaken the baseball patrons will see the best ball ever played next season, and it will be played by the Brotherhood men."

After signing the contract, Kelly received congratulations from his friends. In all the resorts up town frequented by "cranks" this action was the topic of conversation. Many who have had their doubts about the success of the new organization changed their minds when they learned that the Brotherhood had secured the "King of the Diamond." Dunlap and Maul have recently signed contracts, and the Brotherhood people are trying to get Pinkney and Terry of Brooklyn. Bierbauer, the clever little second baseman of the Athletics, is a Brotherhood man, and Larkin, the heavy-hitting first baseman of the same team, wants to join. It is said on good authority that Corkhill of Brooklyn will not play with the Bridegrooms. He signed a contract to play with the American Association, but now that his club has joined the League he does not feel disposed to carry out the requirements of the document. He, too, wants to get on a Brotherhood team.

Al Johnston of Cleveland, the head centre of the financial backers of the Baseball Brotherhood, arrived in this city yesterday. He has visited all the clubs that are to comprise the new league, and states that he is highly gratified with the present outlook. Everywhere, he claims, the backers of the new scheme are jubilant, and they feel confident of success. Players, he says, are being engaged very rapidly, and with few exceptions the men have kept their agreement.

"When the Players' League was proposed," he said, "I was under the impression that we could not get more than half of the League players to take part in the enterprise. Under the skillful management of Ward, Hanlon, Pfeffer, and others, however, the men fell in line, and to-day the prospects are that we will have four-fifths or over of the old players. To add to those we have the pick of the American Association, and you can rest assured that the new league will be stronger by long odds than the old one. Such men as Stovey, Griffin, Kilroy, Comiskey, Robinson, Latham, and dozens of others in the Association whom I might name are in sympathy with us, and some have already signed contracts. We recognize only contracts, and pay no attention whatever to the reserve rule. No player who has signed a contract has been approached, but we have induced men to break the reserve rule, because we don't believe it is lawful. In fact, we have got the opinion of several eminent lawyers on that subject.

"Now as regards deserters," he continued, "I don't care to say much. I would like to allow them to pass by unnoticed, but my colleagues are not disposed to follow my instructions. Some of the men who have signed contracts to play in the old League are at present under contract with the Brotherhood's League. I may cite the case of McKean, the short stop of Cleveland. He not only put his signature to a Brotherhood agreement, but he signed a personal contract with me to play in the new Cleveland Club. Now, I don't propose to let McKean slip out of my grasp if I can help it. I will take the matter to the courts and fight it to the bitter end. For Glasscock, Denny, Boyle, and other deserters I cannot find words in the English language strong enough to express my contempt."

President Ward will arrive here to-day. He has been on a tour of the different cities, and on his travels induced many players to sign contracts. On Dec. 10 a meeting will be held in the Fifth-Avenue Hotel and officers of the Players' League will be elected.

Boston Globe. March 2, 1890

SPALDING INTERVIEWED.

He Tells of that Big Offer to King Kelly of Boston.

President A. G. Spalding returned from New York Thursday looking at peace with himself and all the world. There was no shadow on his countenance to indicate deep-seated chagrin at the failure of his alleged mission — to lure back the only Michael Angelo Kelly of the Chicago club, says the Times of that city.

"What was the object of my visit to the metropolis?" said Mr. Spalding in answer to a question. "I see by the papers that is was to sign Kelly."

"Is it true that you offered Michael $5,000?"

"You don't think for a moment that I would insult so prominent a player by a tender of such a paltry sum? Oh, no! In the ordinary course of business I would not stop at a deal of $1000, $100, or even $1, but when I deal with ball-players it is different. Mr. Kelly is worth $100,000 a year or nothing, and Mr. Kelly is painfully aware of this fact. Ball-players come high, but we must have 'em. And they are worth all they get, too. Of course, when it comes down to a president of the United States, or something ordinary like that, it's different. Presidents only get $50,000 per annum, but ball-players — oh! they would scorn such an offer. If the Chicago club made Mr. Kelly an offer at all it was up in the six figures, with club, stock, goods, chattels, etc., thrown in."

"How about that offer of $1,000,000 for the league's franchise?"

"It was made to President Day, and if the bidders mean business I guess they can be accommodated. The general opinion, however, is that it was a huge bluff. Another base ball fake, you know. Such stories are becoming so numerous that it is difficult to keep track of them. Why, only yesterday it was reported that we had offered Mr. Kelly $15,000; that the American association and players' league were going to combine, and that Mark Baldwin wanted to desert the brotherhood and return to Columbus. In all those stories I do not believe there was one grain of truth."

"What is the sentiment in the East regarding the membership of the national league?"

"There is a growing feeling to the effect that but eight clubs should form the circuit of 1890.

"I did not say so. Neither Indianapolis nor Washington will be frozen out, but whatever arrangement is made will be satisfactory to all parties, you can depend upon that."

Boston Daily Globe. August 5, 1890

GIFT TO KING KELLY.

Enveloped in a maze of spreading branches of beautiful elm and rock maple trees, in a quiet corner of the quiet town of Hingham, stands the elegant residence to be presented to M. J. Kelly, the famous ball player.

On Main st., about a mile from the railroad station, toward the South Hingham village, it sets back from the street, presenting an attractive, homelike appearance.

A high bank wall faces the street with a frontage of 180 feet, broken only by the broad approaches to the residence. A footpath, wide and level, approaches the front of the house, which fronts to the rising sun.

On the south side, 50 feet distant from the footpath, a broad driveway, lined by maples, makes its circling way, ending at the stable and side entrance.

The broad lawn, graded and level as a floor, extends from the street embankment to the house elevation.

The picturesqueness and natural beauty of the surroundings are heightened by the rising land and distant elevation in the rear of the two-acre plot with which the house is surrounded. From the rear of the house the land gently slopes and rises, and where it reaches the water level a small stream courses its way toward the ocean. So much for the surroundings of the residence.

The house itself, as shown in the accompanying illustration, is modern in style and arrangements. Two and one-half stories high, with pitch roof L and stable connected, raised well from the lawn a broad, cool and shaded piazza extends across the entire frontage approached by a flight of wild granite steps.

On the south side, by the driveway, bow windows jut in a picturesque manner and a second smaller piazza extends its tempting invitation to the weary.

The stable is in keeping with the style of the house, with a wide door and ample capacity. To the rear of the barn, with the creek flowing beneath it is a small out-building equipped as a bowling alley, with complete furnishings. A second out-building, standing to the northward near the creek, with slat fencings, is a hennery with ample capacity for a large brood of egg producers.

The rising ground west of the creek at present makes a well-yielding garden patch. The house and stable wear a coat of tinted paint freshly applied and pleasing to the eye.

Entering the house by the front door, admission is had to a large hallway from which rises a broad circling staircase to the second floor.

Doors lead to a neat library with its bow window and ample light and to large double parlors with folding door, bow windows and high ceilings.

Next adjoining on the ground floor is the spacious dining-room, with bow windows and a French glass door opening to the south piazza. A large brick fireplace is a feature of this room.

Connected with the dining-room the kitchen is large and conveniently arranged. In the L, which connects with the stable, a large room is equipped for laundry uses. In addition to the foregoing on the ground floor large closets, a pantry and side rooms are spacious and numerous.

Beneath a large, double cellar, cool and dry, contains dairy arrangements and bins for storage of coal to supply the great furnace, whose heating pipes reach to the ground floor rooms.

The second story is arranged very nearly like the ground floor. The sleeping rooms are six in number, large and high studded, with many windows.

A bathroom and large storage closets are additional features. The garret is roomy, and has one finished room for the use of domestics. The stable is provided with capacity for storage of carriages, a hay loft and stalls for horses and cattle.

During the past few days carpenters, electricians and painters have been busily engaged, and when the presentation day arrives the last nail will have been driven, the last daub of paint will be on and the electric lights will be in position to illuminate "Kell's" new home.

New York Times. June 27, 1891

"KING" KELLY IN A RAGE.

St. Louis, Mo., June 26.— The 3,500 persons who were at Sportsman's Park to-day witnessed an exhibition of temper by "King" Kelly that they won't forget for a long time. The trouble manifested itself in the first inning and was due altogether to Robinson, who attempted to trip O'Neill when he tried to run down to third from second on a throw-in of Seery's. The latter caught Comiskey's high fly and threw to Kelly, who was playing third, to head off O'Neill. Robinson put his foot in front of the runner just as he started, and the trick was seen by the umpire, who declared O'Neill "safe" from Kelly, who met him six feet from the bag. This caused the "King" to become so angry that he fired the ball over the fence.

O'Neill and Lyons, who had obtained a base on balls, trotted home. A few moments later, when play was resumed, Kelly went behind the bat. He kept up a running fire of abuse on Davis, and the latter in a loud voice remarked that he would fine him $25.

"Fine away," said Kelly; "make it $100, it's all the same to me."

"Get out of the game," shouted Davis.

"If I go, my men go too," replied Kelly, and he at once called them off the field.

Everybody was excited, and the situation looked serious, when President Von der Ahe come forward and prevailed upon Kelly to go on with the game.

Brooklyn Eagle. July 6, 1891

KELLY KICKS

And Makes a Disgraceful Exhibition of Himself.

Yesterday's Game at Ridgewood Park Attended by a Crowd of Nearly Five Thousand Persons, Who Become Disgusted at the Tactics of the Captain of Cincinnati's American Association Team.

King Kelly and his aggregation of ball tossers from Cincinnati made a disgusting exhibition of themselves before a crowd of nearly five thousand lovers of the national game at Ridgewood park yesterday. Kelly himself acted like a man half intoxicated and played miserably in the first inning. Behind the bat he was unable to hold the ball, giving way to Hurley in the second inning and taking his place at first base. Crane, who pitched for the New York team last year and was released, was advertised to pitch, but he had been in the sunshine too long and he had to be convoyed to his hotel in a coach. Another man was in an even worse condition than Crane, and was stretched out at full length across the seat of the carriage.

The spectators were the usual crowd of Brooklyn and New York base ball cranks, prone to cheer everybody and applaud everything that is interesting. There were mingled cheers and hisses when Kelly took his position behind the bat in the first inning. He could not hold a ball, and in trying to catch the ball, which no doubt multiplied as it approached him, he repeatedly fell. His antics called forth expressions of contempt from the bleacheries, whose remarks of "Slide, Kelly, slide," and "Put on you glasses, Mike," as he fell around the plate in a vain endeavor to field the ball, must have been edifying to him in the extreme. It was owing to his errors that nine of the Ridgewood team faced Dwyer in the first inning and five runs were tallied.

Seery and Andrews of last year's Brooklyn players' league team were hardly remembered by the spectators and were allowed to face young O'Neil without recognition. Seery got his base on balls and went to second on Andrews' single. Seery, however, was caught napping at third. Kelly was hissed and cheered as he swaggered to the plate. It was noticed that he was out of sorts and seemed not to care whether the game progressed or not. When the umpire called a strike he looked angry. Shouts of "Strike him out, O'Neil," caused him to become wild with rage, and when the second strike was called he yelled at the top of his voice, "I'll kill that pitcher of yours before the game is out." Whether he meant to knock him out of the box or otherwise is left to the readers, but the sally was laughed at and hissed by many spectators. Kelly struck out and Conavan retired on a short infield hit.

The plucky playing of the Ridgewoods won them many friends, and everybody seemed now in their favor. Kelly drank a glass of seltzer and began to play better ball. He changed places with Hurley, who played first base, Hurley going behind the bat. He still kept up his kicking, and it seemed plain that he was trying to bulldoze Umpire Berryman, but didn't succeed. The Ridgewoods were easily retired in the second. As the Cincinnatis came in from the field Kelly took up a position among a crowd of spectators back of the catcher and near the bar. Umpire Berryman ordered him to the players' bench and he refused. The game was stopped and a wordy war ensued between the two men. A crowd gathered around Kelly and he swaggered in among the small boys with all the greatness of his 200 pounds of avoirdupois. He refused to get out, and Manager Wallace of the Ridgewoods came around to reason with him, telling the great Kelly that the people had paid to see a game and not an exhibition of his childishness. Kelly said he did not care, and then the people on the grand stand took a hand in the fun.

"Give him a house in Brooklyn," said one.

"Go on and sit on the players' bench, where you belong," said another.

"We didn't pay to see any monkey shines on your part. Play ball or give us our money back," shouted a third.

"Go and get your money and get out," responded Mike.

"Say, Mike, play ball. Don't make a baby of yourself."

"Oh, I'm 21, young fellow," answered the king, and he made a movement with his big fists.

"Go on, Mike, play ball, we're with you," shouted a couciliating party, but Mike was not in that mood.

"You're giving me the old guy, old boy; I won't take that," was his response.

It seemed as if nothing could move him, but he finally left of his own accord and took a seat on the grass back of first base, and coached his players, surrounded by a crowd of admiring small boys.

The game progressed favorably after that, but Kelly continued to kick without any provocation. The Cincinnatis did some better playing after that and gradually forged ahead, winning finally by the small margin of 8 to 6. The Ridgewoods played a remarkable fielding game, while the Cincinnatis juggled the ball in fine style. Clare, who was injured on the Crescent athletics club grounds recently, played a magnificent game at second base, and Keeler made several fine stops and throws from third. O'Neil pitched well. Sutter was presented with a bouquet of flowers by his friends. Robinson played his old St. Louis trick in the fourth, when he held Clare on second base after he had muffed the ball, and when Clare started for third fielded him out.

Among the spectators was Dave Orr, the popular first baseman, who walked with the aid of a cane. Bob Ferguson, the umpire, was also present. There were many outspoken remarks about Kelly and his tactics, and it is safe to say that he will not attract half as many people should he come to play in Brooklyn again. Score:

CINCINNATI	*R.*	*1B.*	*P.O.*	*A.*	*E.*	*RIDGEWOOD*	*R.*	*1B.*	*P.O.*	*A.*	*E.*
Seery, r. f.	1	0	0	0	0	Nelson, r. f.	1	2	2	0	0
Andrews,l. f.	1	1	2	0	0	Smith, lb.	1	0	7	0	0
Kelly, c. lb.	2	2	10	4	2	Martin, s. s.	1	0	0	2	0
Conavan, s. s.	0	0	2	3	0	Keeler, 3b.	0	2	2	2	0
Robinson, 2b.	2	0	1	3	1	Jones, c.	0	1	6	1	0
Johnston, c. f.	2	2	4	2	0	Hammill, c. f.	1	1	3	0	0
Hurley, lb., c.	0	0	0	0	2	Suiter,l. f.	1	1	1	0	0
Whitney, 3b.	0	1	0	2	1	Clare, 2b.	0	2	2	2	1
Dwyer, p	0	2	2	0	1	O'Neill, p.	1	1	1	0	0
Total	8	8	27	14	7	Total	6	10	24	7	1

SCORE BY INNINGS.

1	2	3	4	5	6	7	8	9

Cincinnati	0	2	0	1	3	0	0	2	[0}
Ridgewood	5	0	0	0	0	0	0	1	0

Earned runs — Cincinnati, 2. Home run — Kelly. Three base hits — Kelly, Whitney. Two base hits — Nelson (2), Jones. Stolen bases — Dwyer, Johnson (2), Clare, Keeler. First base on balls — By Dwyer, 2; by O'Neill, 7. First base on errors — Cincinnati, 1; Ridgewood, 4. Double plays — Johnson and Kelly; Jones and Keeler. Passed ball — Kelly. Wild pitch — Dwyer. Struck out — By Dwyer, 8; by O'Neil, 1. Umpire — Mr. Berryman. Time —1 hour and 55 minutes.

A game which was exciting up to the sixth inning was played Saturday afternoon at the Young Men's Christian Association grounds, Manhattan crossing, between the eastern district association team and the Iroquois club. The former won by heavy batting, aided by the costly errors of the visitors. Hoage pitched a steady game and struck out fourteen men. Wheeler played good ball at times, but his errors were frequent. Totten's fielding and batting were a feature, and the home club showed up in better shape all around than heretofore. The score:

E.D.Y.M.C.A.	*R.*	*1B.*	*P.O.*	*A.*	*E.*	*IROQUOIS*	*R.*	*1B.*	*P.O.*	*A.*	*E.*
Totten, s.s.	5	3	2	5	0	Benny, 1.f.	2	1	2	0	0
Rooch, 2b.	4	2	0	2	0	Wheeler, s.s.p.	2	1	2	8	5
Hoage, p.	0	2	0	0	1	Packard, c. f.	0	0	1	0	0
Ross, c. f.	1	2	0	0	0	Mansan, 1b.	1	2	8	1	2
Thompson, 3b.	1	2	0	3	1	Brook'y, p.s.s.	0	0	1	0	0
Teare, r. f.	1	1	0	0	0	Lau'h'm'r, r.f.	0	0	0	0	0
Mills, 1b.	2	0	11	2	1	Couch, 2b.	2	1	3	0	3
Finkle,1. f.	2	1	1	0	0	McFarline, c.	2	0	3	4	0
H'm'lrelch, c.	2	2	13	1	2	W. Day, 2b.	2	0	4	1	3
Total	18	15	27	13	5	Total	11	5	24	14	13

SCORE BY INNINGS.

1	2	3	4	5	6	7	8	9

The Washington Post. August 26, 1891

KING KELLY AN ISSUE

His Jump to the National League Prolongs the Baseball War.

THE PEACE CONGRESS IN SESSION

Harmonious Proceedings Disturbed by a Sensational Message from Boston-Prospects Now Seem Poor for an Adjustment of Differences.

The peace conference of the League and Association committees, which was in session at the Arlington all day yesterday, broke up in a row about half an hour after midnight. The cause of the trouble was a dispatch received from Boston that Mike Kelly had deserted the Boston Association team and jumped to the League. The information was received in a special dispatch to The Post and was at once communicated to the members of the American Association committee. When the report was soon afterward corroborated from other sources there was an uproar.

Just previously Chairman Kramer had put the question to the joint committee, "That all players now playing or on the pay-roll of each and every club shall remain despite any previous contracts," and the vote was unanimous.

Then came the thunderbolt in the shape of the report that Kelly had jumped. At once the Association contingent was up in arms, and the chairman demanded, on behalf of the Association, that the League committee pledge the return of Kelly to the Boston Association committee, after expressing themselves regarding the fact that the League members had come to the meeting with full power to act and still refused to pledge Kelly's return, on the ground that they were not officially informed, withdrew from the conference.

The Post reporter was acquainted with the facts by the three members of the Association, and President Kramer wanted it distinctly understood that the League had been the first to make any overtures for a conference. The Association people will remain in the city this morning, and if the League committee desire another conference; a written guarantee will be required that Kelly shall be returned before another session will be held.

It was by far the most important baseball conclave of the year and the first meeting of the warring factions since the celebrated breakaway early in the spring. That it was recognized as of the highest importance was evidenced by the number of magnates who were in attendance. National League men and American Association men were here in force, and it was the general talk that something tangible would result from the conference. All the season efforts have been made to bring the two great bodies together, and the meeting was the result of the indefatigable efforts of John T. Brush, the little Napoleon of baseball. Brush has seen practically demonstrated the ruinous course which has been pursued, and has been laboring for a long while to pave the way to a peaceful settlement. The meeting yesterday at the Arlington Hotel was the outcome of his efforts. Through his manipulations the League was induced to make the first overture, and as the League's accredited agent he succeeded in obtaining the Association's consent to a conference.

At the recent Association meeting in St. Louis a committee was appointed to co-operate with a similar committee of the League. These committees were given full power to act for their respective organizations, and whatever decision which might be reached were to be understood to be binding. Messrs. Kramer, president of the Association, Phelps, attorney for the same body, and Von der Ahe, president of the St. Louis Club, were delegated to look after the Association's interests, while the League contingent consisted of John T. Brush, president of the Cincinnati Club; John A. Hart, president of the Chicago Club, and Charles H. Byrne, President of the Brooklyn Club.

These representative committees were empowered to settle all differences in an amicable manner.

Early yesterday morning the Association magnates began arriving. Chris Von Der Ahe came in with his St. Louis club and registered at the Randall. Soon afterward Zach Phelps and President Louis Kramer arrived from Louisville and Cresson Springs, respectively. Then President Von der Horst and Manager Barnie came over form Baltimore, and were soon joined by J. Earle Wagner, from Philadelphia. Julian B. Hart, president of the Boston Association club, was the next to show up, while Manager Gus Schmelz, of the Columbus Club, also came to time. President Bennett and Directors M. B. Scanlon and Sutherland, of the National Club, also reported, and every club but Milwaukee was represented. The different Association magnates were in good spirits, but there was determination not to submit to any "throw-down" by the League.

In the forenoon there was an informal conference, and the stand of the Association was outlined. It was resolved that they would not recede from their former declared position, which was that the only peace desired was respect for the reserve clause, and an interchange of exhibition games. The ground was taken that the League had sought the conference, and it would have to advance a proposition.

After the informal talk the Association people waited until 3 o'clock, the hour appointed for the conclave. When the time arrived Messrs. Kramer, Phelps, and Von der Ahe bundled into a cab, and were driven to the Arlington. The remaining magnates were content to remain at Willard's and await developments. Half an hour passed, and then the committee returned with the news that the other side had failed to materialize. Chris Von der Ahe exhibited a telegram from Charley Byrne to the effect that the train was late, and the League representatives would be on hand at 4 o'clock.

It was just about the latter when a cab passed up the Avenue containing the League people on their way to the Arlington. The Association contingent had determined not to again visit the meeting place unless called on, and accordingly waited.

They had not long to wait, however, as pretty soon Charley Byrne, the national Brooklynite, and Jim Hart, the Windy City man, came walking down to the camp of the enemy. This evidence of good feeling operated on Jack Phelps, who pushed forward and met them. A general handshake followed, and the formal mister was dropped for first names. It was truly a pleasing sight, and the cordial greetings were appreciated by all interested.

Then the picked representatives of the opposing clans proceeded to the Arlington and went into executive session. While the conclave was on the other Association people where occupied in discussing the outcome. The consensus of opinion was that the Association people could better afford continued warfare than the League. J. Earle Wagner said: "Why, every move toward peace has come from the League. We are satisfied to go along our way. We have demonstrated to our satisfaction that we can get along without the League.

"The latter is losing money, and is anxious to make up, we are willing for peace, but is must be at our terms." The others echoed similar sentiments, and it was plainly evident that the Association people appreciated the fact that they held the key to the situation.

"We are not anxious for peace, only to have respect for contracts and play exhibition games," said Billy Barnie. "The Association will most positively refuse," he continued, "to vacate Boston or any other city, and we will hold the right to charge whatever admission we please to our games."

The committee remained in session until 7 o'clock, and President Kramer was, on motion of Mr. Brush, made president of the meeting, and, on motion of Mr. Phelps, James A. Hart was made secretary. The time was spent in a general discussion of the situation toward ascertaining the wishes of the two organizations as to the desirability of framing a new agreement and to the varied features of such an agreement toward protecting the interests of all clubs of the two associations. The committee reported that what was done would have a very material effect upon the future of the national game, and it was necessary to go slow and take ample time to discuss the many new features which have been presented. In consideration of these facts the committee sent down word that the session would be prolonged and nothing officially made known until to-day. Later came the row over Kelly's desertion and the abrupt termination of the conference.

It had been intended to hold a special meeting of the American Association to receive the report of its committee, but the protracted conference interfered with this plan and caused an indefinite postponement.

There was a number of newspaper correspondents awaiting the result of the baseball conference, and when the fact that Mike Kelly had jumped to the League was made known Tim Murnane, the ex-ball player and present sporting editor of the Boston Herald, said: "Well, this will kill Kel. He owes his great success to newspaper notoriety, and his action will cause all the newspaper men to be down on him. He will be dead to the world before another year. Kelly's great popularity was due to his sticking up for the Brotherhood and afterward for the Association; but now that he has weakened he will soon be dead to the world."

Chicago Daily Tribune. August 26, 1891

THERE IS NONE LIKE HIM.

King Kelly to Join the Boston League Club at Once — Consideration $25,000.

Boston, Mass., Aug. 25,—[Special.]—Mike Kelly transferred his allegiance today from the American Association to the National League and signed an iron-clad contract with the Boston club. By this now arrangement

Kelly will act as Captain of the Boston league club for the remainder of the season of 1891 and for the seasons of 1892 and 1893. And for so doing he will receive the sum of $25,000. This $25,000 includes a bonus which is placed by some as high as $10,000. Kelly will play every day, either behind the bat or in the field.

The deal, it seems, has been brought around by Director Conant and George W. Floyd, the theatrical manager. Floyd is a bosom friend of Kelly and has been very anxious to see the latter return to the fold of the league. Director Conant of the Boston League also has been anxious to have Kelly back, as he regards him as a great drawing card. Kelly himself, so his friends say, has not been averse to donning the Boston League uniform for some time, and he has put himself in positions where he could be invited to take his old place. President Soden and Director Billings of the club, however, have thought little of Kelly, and so have opposed negotiations with him. Through Mr. Conant's influence the latter was induced to yield his opinions. President Soden, however, held firm until this afternoon, when he said that if Kelly had no other contracts which would hold him he would agree to offer him a position in the Boston nine.

Kelly has played with the Boston association a week since the disbandment of the Cincinnati club, but he, it seemed, had no contract with the association. The result was the league contract was arranged as above outlined and Mike was not slow to offer his signature to it. Nash is only too glad to be relieved of the duties as Captain, so he says, so no ill-feeling is likely to result in making Kelly his successor. Kelly will leave tomorrow for Cleveland and begin playing at once. The news of Kelly's change was hinted at the game this afternoon, but the officials would not confirm it until this evening.

Chicago Daily. August 27, 1891

SPLIT OVER KING KELLY.

The League—Association Peace Conference Comes To Naught.

The Von der Ahe Crowd Demanded That the Mighty Michael Be Returned to the Boston Association Club Instanter—The League People

Fail to Respond Satisfactorily, and the White-Winged Dove Immediately Quits the Scent — President Kramer Resigns.

WASHINGTON, D. C., AUG. 26.—[SPECIAL.]—There was no meeting of the baseball magnates at the Arlington Hotel today but there was submitted from the representatives of the American Association a communication to the effect that the Kelly deal at Boston had nullified all previous work of the committee and that a further conference would be impossible between the leaders of the two factions unless Kelly was ordered back to the association team at Boston. This communication was signed by President Kramer who at a meeting of his association held here this afternoon tendered his resignation to take effect Sept. 1. This was accepted after a vote of thanks had been tendered and Zack Phelps of Louisville was chosen to succeed Mr. Kramer for the remainder of the baseball season. Subsequently the representatives of the National League replied to the document of their opponents in which they set out the various propositions submitted for consideration and suggested that the Kelly matter be placed on a similar footing. They would wait for another conference until 5 o'clock in the afternoon. None of the American Association people put in an appearance, however, and the peace overtures are off indefinitely.

Kramer's Ultimatum.

Following is a copy of the letter sent this morning by Mr. Kramer to the representatives of the league:

> Gentlemen: We in good faith accepted your proposition for a "peace conference," and in it attended with the intention and disposition to make an earnest effort to settle all existing differences in some manner which would be honorable both to your people and ours alike. While we were thus engaged within a conference looking to a fair and honorable settlement we were apprised of the fact that one of your clubs had (we trust without your knowledge, consent, or permission) entered our ranks and induced one of our players to "jump" his contract. You will, of course, agree that in view of this conference, which was well known to all your club members who had authorized you to represent them, any such action was not in good faith, but was a positive violation of the letter and spirit of the negotiations which had passed between us.
>
> In view of this we feel that we cannot properly continue our negotiations until your people have shown a disposition to meet and treat fairly. Unless, therefore, you can guarantee to us the return of the player mentioned and good faith in our negotiations and dealings we shall be compelled to withdraw entirely from the conference.
>
> Louis Kramer.

The following is the reply to the league's representatives:

Gentlemen: We are in receipt of your communication of this date. By mutual consent and in good faith the National League appointed a committee of three to meet a like committee from the American Association for the purpose of harmonizing any differences existing between the two organizations. After organizing your committee representing the American Association submitted the following demands as a basis for settlement:

Association Demands.

1. The reversal of the decision of the National Board in the cases of Stovey and Bierbauer and the remanding of said players to the Athletic club of the American Association.
2. That all players now under contract with the American Association be subject to reservation by the association as may hereafter be provided.
3. That the legality of the contracts of Vickery and Schriver with the Chicago club be subject to discussion.
4. That all players who have signed two contracts shall be suspended.
5. That the National Board as now constituted be abolished.
6. The adoption of a new national agreement or compact.
7. That the Western Association be denied admission as a major party to such new agreement.
8. That the American Association circuit shall be composed of Chicago, Brooklyn, Cincinnati, Boston, Philadelphia, St. Louis, Baltimore, Washington, Columbus, Louisville, and Milwaukee.
9. That the right of the American Association to maintain clubs in said cities shall be perpetual, that is to say, in case any club should resign its membership, disband, or be expelled, the American Association shall have the right at any time to establish another club in such city.

Von der Ahe's Men Bolt.

We were discussing these demands when your committee withdrew for conference. Upon your return you announced that early in the evening you had been in possession of the information that a player claimed by an association club had been signed by a National League club, and that such information had just been confirmed. Mr. Phelps then stated that the hour being late it would be well to adjourn, and upon motion we did adjourn to meet at 10 o'clock this morning. As far as we are informed nothing has occurred since the hour of adjournment to change the situation as existing at that time. At 10 o'clock this morning we were at the place of meeting prepared to proceed with the business which brought us here. After waiting some time your communication was received, in which you make the following additional demand — viz.:

"Unless, therefore, you, the League committee, can guarantee to us the return of the player mentioned, and good faith in our negotiations and dealings we shall be compelled to withdraw entirely from the conference."

We respectfully submit that this last demand occupies precisely the same status as any of the other demands above mentioned, and is a proper subject for discussion in joint conference. We are here for the purpose of discussing and adjusting, if possible, any and all differences between the two organizations, and are prepared to proceed in compliance with our understanding at time of adjournment last night. We, therefore, hold ourselves in readiness to meet you, and will remain here until 5 o'clock this afternoon, unless otherwise advised.John T. Brush,

C. H. Byrne,
James A. Hart.

Do Not Want the King.

BOSTON, MASS., AUG. 26.—The directors of the Boston Baseball club of the American Association say that nothing will be done about the jump of Kelly. Today they sent a telegram to President Kramer asking that the Kelly matter be not considered in the conference at Washington. They do not need him and would have no use for him, even if he were returned. The club would not make the slightest move to get him back. There would be no proceedings against him or the clubs that enticed him away.

Manager Bancroft of the Milwaukees said that Kelly came to him upon entering the grounds yesterday afternoon and told him what he had done and that he had signed a contract for the remainder of this season and the beginning of next for $20,000, $13,500 down, besides a ticket to Europe for himself and his wife. Mr. Bancroft said that President Von der Ahe of the St. Louis Browns could have signed Kelly in St. Louis on the last trip of the Cincinnati's association nine. Kelly signified his willingness to sign with Von der Ahe. It was Von der Ahe's intention to play him in left field and behind the bat and next year to place him at the head of the Chicago American Association nine. Kelly afterward changed his mind and said he wanted to play in Boston. Von der Ahe interposed no objection and asked if he could go right away. He took the train that same night for Boston. That the Boston Association nine could not sell out is shown by the fact that President Kramer holds a deed of trust for 51 per cent of the capital stock of the club. Even were this not so the association would keep a club in Boston on new grounds were the present club disposed of in any way.

Boston Daily Globe. November 9, 1894

DEATH OF KELLY.

Baseball Giant Gives in to Pneumonia.

Had Been Ill Since Monday When He Came Here.

His Plans Were to Play at a Boston Theater.

History of "King's" Career on Many Diamonds.

Anson Pays a Tribute to His Partner of Old.

At 9.55 last night "King Kelly" heard the decision of the Great Umpire from which there is no appeal. The famous ball player passed away at that hour at the emergency hospital, with a few of his old friends watching every phase of his last uphill fight in the game where defeat is sure.

So died "Kel" of pneumonia, in the city of his greatest triumphs. He came to Boston, where he has been idolized as few ball players have, and though his last work has been done far from here yet his deathbed was in this city and among the people he loved so well.

He came here Monday from his home at Paterson, N J, to play an engagement at the Palace theater. He caught a slight cold on the boat from New York, but thought little of it. He went to the Plymouth house, the proprietor of which is an old friend of his and a brother Elk. Mr. Anderson noticed that Mike was not well, and put him to bed at once. The slight cold, aided by the east wind and murky chill of last Monday, were too much for the player, and he grew worse so rapidly that Dr. Galvin, another old and dear friend, took him to the emergency hospital, and gave up his private room to him.

About 3 o'clock yesterday he was very low, and the doctor called in a physician from the city hospital. The patient rallied about 5 o'clock and the last sacraments of the church were administered by Fr Hickey of St James' church. After this he rallied a little more, but soon began to sink again, and continued to do so until the hour above stated, when he was called out for the last time.

He has a brother, John, at Troy, N Y, and a wife and child in Paterson, N J. His wife was sent for yesterday, but did not arrive in time to see her husband alive.

There will be many sorrowing and sympathetic friends all over the United States this morning, for Mike Kelly was loved for the unyielding pluck and courage with which he did his work. Among his mates and his profession he left not one enemy. He was a welcome figure on any ball field, and a familiar one from Portland, Me, to San Francisco, Calif.

Old men and young, bankers, brokers, statesmen, clergymen, lawyers, physicians have applauded him, with the American small boy.

Mike Kelly, the beau ideal of a ball player, shrewd, skillful, and so quick-witted that his work was always a wonder and a delight, will be missed by the baseball public. They will say: "Take him for all in all, we never shall see his like again."

Michael J. Kelly was born in Troy, N Y, in 1857. His career as a ball player began with the Haymakers of Troy, N Y, in 1873, with whom he played right field until 1875. His first professional engagement was in 1876 and 77 with the Olympics of Paterson, and in 1878 he played with the Buckeyes of Columbus, O, McCormack pitching. In 1879 he was right fielder and change catcher for the Cincinnati league team, and was considered the best catcher in the profession. In the fall of 1879 he went with the Cincinnati-Chicago combination to California, where he was engaged by the Chicagos as change catcher and right fielder. Feb 14, 1887, he was sold to Boston for $10,000 by the president of the Chicago club.

The first trips of the Boston team after Mike Kelly joined it will probably never be forgotten by those who participated in them. The release of the "only" had just been purchased by the Boston club for the magnificent sum of $10,000. The check sent by A. G. Spalding was photographed and used for advertising purposes, and in some of the cities the dead walls and show boards were placarded with pressing invitations to "Come and see the great Kelly," "Don't miss the ten thousand dollar beauty" and other inspiring legends. Kelly himself suggested the "beauty" attachment, inasmuch as he one day announced to the occupants of the bleacheries, with whom he was engaged in one of those wordy warfares that are so characteristic of the man: "O, I'm a beaut; you can bank on that — a regular $10,000 beauty. I come high, but they had to have me."

Up to that time, 1887, no player had ever received the advertising and booming given to Mike Kelly. All Boston expected him to win the championship by himself, and were greatly disappointed when he didn't do it. For all that he played great ball for the club.

"Kel's" first appearance abroad in a Boston uniform was at Baltimore, in the spring of 1887. The Bostons played four exhibition games there, which were exciting and interesting. Barnie's grounds (not the present park) were taxed to their capacity on the first day. The local papers called the crowd 10,000. It was a tremendous crowd anyway for Baltimore, and every man and boy present wanted the home club to win. They cheered Kelly at first, but after he got to quarreling with Capt Tom Burns of the Orioles, and the umpire the crowd jeered the "Only," and guyed him terribly for dropping a couple of easy flies. Mr Barnie "rung in," as Kelly called it, a man named Marshall as umpire, and he robbed the Bostons on every possible occasion. "Kel" wouldn't have him the second day, and got a man who was quite as bad. Boston got two of the games, and would have had all four, despite the umpires, had the balance of the team shown the nerve that Kelly did.

Kelly's first appearance in Chicago was a memorable one. The papers devoted columns to it. There was a tremendous crush at the Leland hotel to see him. The teams went to the grounds in carriages, and the streets along the route were filled with people, and the "king" got cheers enough to flatter his cap to jump from his head. The crowd at the grounds was an immense one. Kelly played great ball, but his team was beaten, and "Mike" himself was stricken with "charley horse."

He ought not to have played the next day, but Anson persuaded him to do so, promising to let him have a runner, a promise he forgot at the most critical stage of the game.

A business firm sent a silver service to the grounds, which was to be given to the captain of the successful team. The service was moved from players' bench to players' bench, according to the score, until "Kel" alleged it was a Jonah, and refused to have it on his side of the diamond.

It seemed "Kel's" property, sure, with Boston three ahead, but Anson saved his bacon by making a home run with the bases full and two out. Then "Kel," not to be outdone, made a three-base hit, bringing in the run that tied the game, and would have won it but for the bad base running of Madden, who was caught napping at third base. In the last inning "Kel" had a chance to win the silver, and really made a hit that would have done it under ordinary circumstances, but having to run for himself, and being awfully slow, Williamson got the ball in left center, and had time enough to run in and throw the "Only" out at first, and the silver went to Anson.

Kelly was a fine looking athlete, standing 5 feet 11¼ inches in hight, and weighing when in condition 180 pounds.

As a batsman, base runner, thrower and a player to take advantage he never had a superior, and in the four good points never had an equal.

In 1886 Kelly led the league batsmen with an average of 370, and though considered one of the finest all-round ball players on the diamond never figured very high in fielding averages, for the reason that he always took too many chances. Mike Kelly's work for the Boston team is familiar to all the lovers of baseball.

When the players broke away from the league in 1890 Kelly was on the side of the players, and remained with them through the season, refusing some very large offers to jump his contract.

In 1891 Kelly preferred the new American association to the league, as they had offered him a very small salary. The Cincinnati club of the association were in need of a captain, and Kelly was transferred to that city. About the middle of August of that season, finding the sledding rough in the queen city, Kelly accepted an offer from the Boston league team for the remainder of the season of 91 and the season of 92. In 1893 Kelly was released to the New York club, and finished the season with that club, but had some trouble with Capt Ward, and finally retired from the league to manage the Allentown club of the Pennsylvania state league.

For the last two winters Kelly went on the variety stage, giving songs and recitations, and was fairly successful. Kelly had a fund of natural wit, and was one of the biggest-hearted fellows in the profession and a universal favorite with his fellow players.

ANSON'S TRIBUTE TO KELLY.
Played Ball for the Good of His Team at Expense of His Own Record.

CHICAGO, NOV. 8—While with the Chicagos Kelly was Anson's right hand man. He acted as change catcher and right fielder. Said Anson tonight: "Kelly invariably played ball for the good of his team, and in this way injured his individual batting, fielding and catching record. It was this self-sacrificing spirit, coupled with a natural quickness of thought and execution, that made him so valuable as a ball player to the clubs he played with. He was a great strategist, well versed in every point of play, and competent to play any position."

New York Times. November 9, 1894

"KING" KELLY DIES OF PNEUMONIA.

The Famous Player's Record on the Baseball Field.

Michael J. Kelly, the famous baseball player, died in the Emergency Hospital, Boston, last night, of pneumonia. He had been ill since Monday, when he had gone to Boston to join the London Gaiety Girls Theatrical Company, in which he was to do small comedy parts.

"King" Kelly, as he was dubbed by the occupants of the bleacheries at baseball games, was born at Troy, N. Y., but when young was taken to Paterson, N. J., where he learned to play baseball. He played with the Olympics of Paterson, and did so well that he soon had the offer of a position among professional players. In 1887 he joined the Buckeye Club of Columbus, of which McCormack, the old-time pitcher, was a member. The next year Kelly played in Cincinnati.

It was in 1880 that Kelly joined the Chicago White Stockings, with whom he made his reputation. He developed into a hard hitter and an excellent catcher. The old batteries, McCormack and Kelly, and afterward Clarkson and Kelly, became well known all over the country. When not catching, Kelly usually played in right field. His stealing of bases won for him the expression, "Slide, Kelly, slide!"

The Boston Baseball Club, in 1887, paid Chicago $10,000 for Kelly's release. It was the first time so large a sum had been paid for a baseball player's services. When the Brotherhood was organized, Kelly left the National League and played for Boston in the players' organization.

In 1892 the New-York club secured Kelly's services. He did not get in good playing condition that season, however. Last season he was Captain of the Allentown nine, in Pennsylvania, and afterward was transferred to Yonkers, in the Eastern League. Kelly was popular among the players, and but for his uncertain habits could undoubtedly have held his place in the National League among the younger players.

Chicago Daily. November 9, 1894

MIKE KELLY IS OUT.

Famous Ball Player Dies of Pneumonia at Boston.

His Illness Short and Death Unexpected — The Fourth of Chicago's Great Team Which Won Five League Championships to Pass Away — Ready-Witted, Careless, and Popular, Kelly Saved Nothing and Lost His Ball Playing Ability at the End.

BOSTON, MASS., NOV. 8. — [SPECIAL.] — Mike Kelly, ex-king to the diamond, died tonight at 9:55 at the Emergency Hospital of pneumonia. A few friends were at his bedside when the end came. Kelly came to Boston Monday from Paterson, N. J., his home, to appear in a local theater, and he caught a slight cold on the boat from New York Sunday night, and on his arrival here Monday went to bed at the Plymouth House. There was a severe storm Monday, and the chilly weather helped develop Kelly's sickness into pneumonia, and he was removed to the hospital Tuesday and began to sink rapidly, with brief rallying periods. This afternoon thc last sacraments of the church were administered by Father Hickey of St. James' Church. Kelly rallied a little, recognized his friends, and then sank into a stupor, from which he was "called out" for the last time.

Kelly's Ball-Playing Career.

Kelly's career began with the Haymakers of Troy in 1873. With them he played right field two years. His first professional engagement was in 1876 and1877 with the Olympics of Paterson. In 1878 he was a member of the Buckeyes of Columbus, O. Then he went to the Cincinnati league team. The Chicago team engaged him in 1880 and for six seasons he played with that club. In 1887 Kelly was sold to Boston. He was with the Bostons till 1890, when he joined the Players' League. In 1891 he captained the Cincinnati Association team. Then he returned to the Boston Reds and later became a member of the Boston League team. He joined the New Yorks in 1893. This year he managed the Allentown, Pa., and Yonkers, N. Y., teams.

Mike Kelly first became famous as right fielder of the Cincinnati Reds of 1879.

From Cincinnati he came to Chicago in 1880 and played in right field and as change catcher for the greatest team the country had seen. It won the championship in 1880, 1881, 1882, 1885, and 1886. Under Anson in those days were: Flint, Corcoran, Larkin, Goldsmith, Dalrymple, Gore, Pfeffer, Williamson, and Tom Burns, all in their prime. The team was a popular idol in and out of Chicago, and made a great deal of money. From Chicago Kelly was sold to the Bostons in 1887, and when the brotherhood movement of 1890 turned up he went with his fellows, and was manager and Captain of the Boston Brotherhood team.

When the Players' League fell to pieces Kelly returned to the Cincinnati club, and the next year to Boston. He and Conant of the Triumvirs were always great friends. Steady dissipation had taken the edge off Kelly's ability, and this season he was not wanted by the league, and, backed by A. L. Johnson, an old friend, played a team of league castoffs, which he called "The Terrors," at Allentown, Pa., and later, at Yonkers, N. Y.

In his prime Kelly was one of the greatest of ball players. He was one of the best of batsmen, and originator of the modern dashing style of baserunning, a really great catcher, full of winning tricks and devices, and a splendid thrower. As an outfielder Kelly was never first-class. But he was always "in the game," ready to take any chance to win, and of great value to a team.

Kelly and Jim McCormick — the once great pitcher — both graduated in baseball from the Paterson, N. J., lots. Kelly was a good looking, stalwart fellow, witty, free living, and reckless in money matters. His wife, as good-natured as himself, steadied Kel a great deal.

Kel Had No Business Ability.

Mike Kelly had no business ability. When managing the Bostons his accounts were curiosities. The writer recalls running against Mike one spring morning in the corridor of the Bay State House at Worchester, Mass. He was wrestling with a small account book and a big carpenter's pencil. To a "What's on, Mike?" Kel answered plaintively: "This bookkeeping's hell, mo boy."

Kelly will hardly ever be forgotten while baseball is played in America. There was no more popular ball player in Chicago than Kelly, and after leaving the team he always hankered to return to it. Though restive of Anson's control Mike respected the old man's sterling qualities and the old man reciprocated. Kelly had won him many games. When he, Corcoran, Goldsmith, and Williamson — Mike's especial crony — were on the old Chicago team it was jolly all night and play good ball, too. Many a gambler lost a big bet after seeing Mike and Corcoran with convivial spirits when the sun rose.

In 1886 a wise knot in Cleveland made a big pool to back the Clevelands against Chicago because Corcoran and Kelly had gone to Weddell House as drunk as lords as the sun was coming up. Then Chicago pitchers worked in turn, and it was Corcoran's turn that afternoon. In the game Corcoran shut the Clevelands out, and not a base hit did its men get. Chicago didn't make many, and got but one run. Kelly drove it in. Of the old team Kelly is the fourth to die. Ned Williamson passed away last winter and Terry Larkin and Frank Flint two years ago. Only Anson and Pfeffer are playing ball.

Kel's Old Clubmates' Sorrow.

Anson, Wilmot, and Pfeffer spoke of Kel last night. Anson seemed almost broken-hearted over Kelly's death.

"Kelly was a general on the diamond, a born humorist, and an agreeable companion," said the old Captain.

"As a batter and base-runner, Mike had few equals, and no man was ever of more value behind the bat. Contrary to the general opinion, he was not a hard man to get along with, and I would willingly have had him on the Chicago team at any time."

"I never played with Kelly," said Wilmot, "but I have often admired his skill, while he always impressed me as a kindly, free hearted, and whole souled gentleman."

"I have played for years with and against Mike Kelly," said Pfeffer. "He was a great catcher, a winning ball player, and a jester of rich and unrivaled humor.

"Off the field he was a jovial spendthrift and a kindly pleasant fellow with all."

"I can't say much," said Jimmy Ryan. "Kel was a good fellow and a champion ball player."

"Another of the old heroes gone," said Jim Hart. "Corcoran, Flint, Williamson, and Kelly now are dead, and Kelly was beyond a doubt the most original character of all. I did not have him here, but he played with me in Boston and I knew him well, both as a player and a man."

Brooklyn Eagle. November 10, 1894

A BASE BALL STAR.

The death of Michael J., more familiarly known as "*Mike" Kelly,* the base ball player, will attract a large share of attention, because he attained great prominence in a form of sport which interests nearly every one. That is not a mistaken judgment which prompts the newspapers to devote as much space to a review of Kelly's career as they would to that of a distinguished theologian or philosopher, for in his way this man was as much of a conspicuous figure as any of those in other planes of life, and certainly he was more popular with the masses. Everybody had heard of him. The measure of his fame on the diamond field was akin to that of men who get to the top in any sphere, and if he did anything to popularize base ball, which must be conceded, the influence which he exerted was of a wholesome and healthy kind. Perhaps more than any other player he showed that it is possible to make as much money in base ball as some of our best lawyers and physicians earn in the practice of their professions, and that, too, while working but a few months in the year. He was one of the leaders in the movement for the brotherhood, which was in every respect a disastrous experiment, but he remained true to it so long as there was any prospect of success in spite of tempting offers to desert its colors. There are those who affect to view with cynicism the fact that a man like Kelly could command a salary of $10,000, but it should be remembered that he was at the head of the list, and that competition in base ball is not less keen than in other branches of endeavor. The time will come when even Kelly's reputation will be discounted by succeeding players, but now that he has gone, it is only fair to accord to him that degree of credit to which he is fairly entitled.

The Washington Post. November 12, 1894

"KING" KELLY LAID AWAY.

Thousands Attend the Funeral of the Famous Baseball Player.

BOSTON, MASS., NOV. 11.—To-day all that was mortal of poor Mike Kelly was gently lowered to the grave by those who had been near and dear to him throughout life. For four hours a steady stream of people filed slowly into the rooms of the Boston Lodge of Elks, of Hayward place, and did the dead man honor. He reposed in a magnificent casket, half buried beneath floral decorations. Around the room were wreaths and crosses and costly pieces of floral work, contributed by friends. Fully 8,000 people were present.

It was nearly 1 o'clock before the throng could be checked, and even then they continued to arrive and block the street. The sidewalks were lined by hundreds waiting to see the funeral cortege go by. Inside were hundreds of the dead man's friends from far and near. The Verdi Quartet rendered in a touching manner "They are gathering homeward in every land" prior to the body being taken to the church. Shortly after 1 o'clock the casket was borne to the hearse outside and driven to St. Joseph's Church, where a brief service was held. After the service the remains were taken to Mount Hope Cemetery, where they were interred according to the rites of the Elks.

Chicago Daily Tribune. June 16, 1918

HOW KING KELLY WON A PENNANT FOR WHITE SOX

Bumps Rival Baseman in Crucial Game in 1881.

BY T. Z. COWLES.
[Sporting Editor Chicago Tribune 1868-'75]

How Mike Kelly came to the Chicago club and how Mike Kelly won a league championship for the Chicago White Stockings is a story worth telling.

Certain it is that to one player—not even Anson himself—ever contributed more of value to the success of the club than did Mike Kelly. In respect of the ginger, the pep, the activity of mind and body, and above all the intense desire to win, it would be hard to name his equal among all the ball players of the last fifty years.

There never was but one "Kel." As batter, base runner, right fielder, and change catcher, he was a gold mine of usefulness to his club. There was one particular field play in which he was more successful than any other right fielder. It was throwing out a man at first base on an apparently safe hit.

Plays for the Batter.

According to his judgment of batters, which was exceptionally correct, he would play deep in his field or half way, as the case might be. On a clean grounder between first and second Kelly would race to meet the ball, pick it up on the run, and by a quick throw get his man at first base. This was smart ball indeed. It was Kelly ball.

It was "Boss" Hulbert's good judgment, backed up by Anson's correct estimate, that brought Kelly to Chicago. But The Tribune had something to do with it, as we shall see. In 1881, when the writer was night editor of The Tribune, and a sporting authority emeritus as it were, the White Stockings were playing against the Cincinnati Reds on the lake front grounds. I was there as a spectator.

Cigar Starts Fanning Bee.

Hulbert came to the press stand, tapped me on the shoulder, and said:

"Don't you want to smoke?"

"Yes," was my answer.

We went over to the right hand bleachers and lighted up. Cincinnati was in the field. The team of that year embraced Deacon White as catcher; Will White, his brother (always wearing gold-bowed spectacles) pitcher; Cal McVey, first base; Pete Hotaling, left field; Dickerson, center; Kelly, right field. No matter about second baseman, short stop and third baseman. They weren't much account anyhow.

"If you had your pick of those fellows out there," said Hulbert, "which would you choose?"

Cowles Picks Kelly.

"There's but one man in the whole bench I'd take as a gift," was my reply.

"Which one?"

"The right fielder. He's worth more than all the rest of the outfit put together."

"That's exactly what I think," said Hulbert.

Kelly was signed to play for Chicago before he left town. There was no reserve rule in operation then. A player could sign with another club at the expiration of his season's contract. Along in the winter Hulbert asked to meet him at lunch. Two men from Cincinnati were waiting for us, by appointment.

They were Justus Thorner, manager of the Reds, and Judge Hendrickson of Cincinnati. They had come to Chicago to beg Hulbert to release Kelly back to their club, and they pleaded earnestly against being compelled to lose their best man. It would hurt their club, they urged, and cut down gate receipts. Hulbert listened patiently to their arguments. Turning to me he said:

"What do you think about it?"

Chicago Needs Kelly.

"Chicago needs Kelly and ought to have him," was my answer. "Cincinnati needs him, too, but will profit more by his absence than by his presence. Baseball receipts in Chicago when it has a winning team are twice or three times the receipts in Cincinnati, win or lose. Cincinnati stands to get more money out of Chicago games than it could hope to get out of home games. Kelly should play with Chicago, by all means."

And it was settled that way.

How Kelly won the league championship for Chicago was this way. It was in 1882, as I remember, that Providence and Chicago were tied in the race and had but one more game to play. That game would decide the championship. They were playing on the lake front grounds.

Radbourne was pitching for Providence, little Gilligan was the catcher, Joe Start the first baseman, and George Wright the shortstop. Harry Wright was the team manager. For Chicago Corcoran was pitcher, Anson first base, and Kelly right field.

The ninth inning found Providence one run ahead — score, 7 to 6. Chicago must get two to win, one to tie. One man was out and one on third base. Kelly had reached first base on a safe hit. Anson at bat. It looked like one run in and a tie at the worst. Kelly was leading off first to coax a throw and give the man on third the chance to score, but Radbourne was too foxy for that. He held Kelly on first long enough for the fatal play that was as follows:

Anson batted a swift ball to the ground and it landed in George Wright's hands on the first bound. A double play, the side out, and the league championship for Providence was what it looked like, George Wright, always rather fond of posing on the ball field, spilled the beans, by the aid of Mike Kelly. With Kelly the game was never out till it was played out. At the crack of the ball from Anson's bat he set sail for second base. Wright had oceans of time, but he chose to make a showy play. His foot on the second base bag and Kelly was out on a force. There was no hurry about firing the ball to Joe Start and completing the double play, as Anson was a rather slow runner.

Kel Bumps George Wright.

But Kelly didn't seme to know when he was out. He kept right on for second base at the gait of an express train and a good deal of its force. Just as Wright had raised his arm to throw to first base Kelly bumped into him pell mell, the ball went fifteen feet over Joe Start's head, and into the bleachers. Anson easily made the circuit, with the man on third ahead of him. The game was won by the White Stockings, 8 to 7, and the league championship was won with it.

Harry Wright made a dreadful kick over Kelly's "interference," but the umpire ruled that Kelly had the right of way on the base line and the two runs were scored.

Ball players of the long ago period were not like their fellows of 1918, born with gold spoons in their mouths. The epoch of princely salaries had not dawned. They traveled in ordinary sleeping cars at night, when they could get them. If not, they sat up. No special Pullmans for them.

Sox Captain's Salary $2,000.

Jimmy Wood, second baseman and captain of the White Stockings of 1870 got $400 a month for five months' play. John McGraw, manager and field captain of the New York Giants, is supposed to receive $30,000 a year. Excepting Wood, no man in the Chicago team of 1870 received more than $300 a month; some of them only $200 a month.

New York Times. June 4, 1938

CASEY A FICTITIOUS FIGURE

Mike (King) Kelly Inspiration of Baseball Epic, Says Reader

To Sports Editor of The New York Times:

May I not contribute my 2 cents' worth to "Casey at the Bat," in the shape of the enclosed copy of a letter I wrote in 1935 at the time of the passing of DeWolf Hopper?

I also have a time-worn, full-page copy of The Evening Mail supplement of May 7, 1904, in which is printed "Casey" in light postures in conformity with the verses of the rhyme, in which the uniform worn is adorned with the legend "Boston."

The heading on the page is "Casey at the Bat as Recited by DeWolf Hopper." There are no "Mudville" verses and the final wind-up in the last verse is:

"But there is no joy in Boston;
Mighty Casey has struck out."

As long ago as 1913, The Mail published a letter by me, similar to the one enclosed, so that "Kelly at the Bat" is not a newly created idea in the mind of the writer.

Significance Is Lost

It isn't a matter of international concern whether it was "Casey" or "Kelly" who struck out, but if, perchance, some rhyme had been written about Babe Ruth, which subsequently became about "Booth," the significance of any such poem would be completely lost without the personality of the Sultan of Swat—and so it is with "Kelly" changed to a phantom "Casey."

Here is my letter of three years ago:

"The death of DeWolf Hopper recalls that his recitation 'Casey at the Bat' was really written around the personality and characteristics of Mike (King) Kelly. 'Kelly at the Bat' was written and published under this title in the late Eighties and it fitted Mike Kelly to a nicety.

"Kelly was as pugnacious and scrappy as he was a prince of catchers and a star batter. He was considerable of a poser and swaggerer, as befitted a ball player for whom Boston paid Chicago $10,000. Because of this and his undoubted ability, he was as much a national figure as Babe Ruth later became.

"Naturally, he was the butt of the crowd at the games and old-timers of fifty years ago or so who attended games at the old Polo Grounds will recall the razzing meted out to King Kelly, which never bothered him to any degree, although he was not averse to using his dukes if occasion arose.

Kelly Among Audience

"It was the custom then for the Casino Theatre to invite the New York and visiting teams to attend its performances in a body. One night, when both the Boston and New York teams were in the audience, DeWolf Hopper, in 'Wang,' recited 'Kelly at the Bat,' substituting 'Casey' for 'Kelly' in order to avoid wounding Mike's sensibilities.

"This recitation gave the rhyme publicity and popularity, which has prevailed up to today. The original poem started off with 'There was ease in Kelly's manner as he stepped up to his place,' but some evil genius prefixed three meaningless verses with reference to a fictitious 'Mudville.'

"Mike Kelly and his contemporaries are all but forgotten, except by the old Polo Grounds habitues, who, like Ben Bolt's Sweet Alice, 'wept with delight' on those exceedingly rare occasions when 'Mighty Kelly struck out,' as he was far more likely to crack out a three-bagger and clear the bases.

Kipling No Baseball Fan

"The popularity of 'Kelly at the Bat' and his national reputation resulted, a little while after the publication of the poem, in a song which also attained wide popularity, viz: 'Slide, Kelly, Slide.' These words are referred to by Rudyard Kipling in 'From Sea to Sea,' but his reference indicates that the eminent author had not the slightest conception of their meaning.

"Substituting 'Casey' for 'Kelly' deprived the rhyme of its chief asset, King Kelly himself, for the story was wound around, and bound up in Mike's actions, postures, personality and uncanny ability.

"When the Springtime comes and we ancient recall the joyous days of the old Polo Grounds, our thoughts revert to this and that diamond here of his day, and memory brings to mind Mike Kelly, his skill and his actions, and we regret that the real hero of the now famous rhyme was displaced by a mythical 'Casey.'"

William Douglas Kilpatrick.
New York, May 30, 1938.

Index

Prepared by Roger Erickson, SABR Bibliography Committee